STRIDE
by
STRIDE

The Illustrated Story of Horseracing

In memory of my mother, Margaret Holland

STRIDE by STRIDE

The Illustrated Story of Horseracing

Anne Holland

'Like leaves before a tempest the flying beauties race,
And there's all the Vale to conquer as you settle down to ride;
Youth's eager fire within you flames at challenge of the pace,
And blood calls to blood, stride by stride.'

From *Forrard On!* by Rancher

Macdonald
Queen Anne Press

A *Queen Anne Press* BOOK

© Anne Holland 1989

First published in Great Britain in 1989 by
Queen Anne Press, a division of
Macdonald & Co (Publishers) Ltd
66–73 Shoe Lane
London EC4P 4AB

A member of Maxwell Pergamon Publishing Corporation plc

Jacket photographs – Front: Mary Evans Picture Library
 Back: Allsport

British Library Cataloguing in Publication Data
Holland, Anne
 Stride by stride: the illustrated story of horseracing.
 1. Racehorses. Racing
 I. Title
 798.4

ISBN 0–356–17496–4

Typeset by J&L Composition Ltd, Filey, North Yorkshire
Printed and bound in Great Britain by Butler and Tanner Ltd, Frome

ACKNOWLEDGEMENTS

The author wishes to thank all those who have
given their time and help in research for this
book, including:
Ascot Racecourse, Alex Bird, Gary Bivens
(Weatherbys Statistical Record), Peter Bromley,
Ray Bulman, Doreen Calder, Arnold Crowhurst
MRCVS, Bruce Daglish (Horse UK), Oliver
Douieb, Epsom Racecourse, Equitrack, John
Ford, Edward Gillespie (Cheltenham Racecourse
Library), Barney Griffiths (British School
of Racing), Geoffrey Hamlyn, Andrew Harrison
(*Sporting Life*), Barry Hills and Peter Hudson, the
late Margaret Holland, Ron Hutchinson, Nick
Lees, Genevieve Murphy (Arab Horse Society),
National Horseracing Museum, National Stud,
John Oaksey, Jonjo O'Neill, John Parrett
(Aintree Racecourse), Jon Scargill, Fiona
Shepherd-Cross, Peter Smiles, David Swannell,
Lady Thomson, John Tosetti, Jeremy Tree,
Paddy Warren, Michael Watt (Tattersall's),
Michael Williams

Picture credits

Allsport: back cover, 54b, 126, 127. Associated Press: 64.
Barnaby's Picture Library: 165, 167. BBC Enterprises: 163.
Blood Horse, Kentucky: 125b. Bridgeman Art Library: 7, 30,
31t/Private Collections; 65t/British Museum. Kenneth Bright:
168. Camera Press: 32, 37; 49/Jane Brown; 68b, 136. Chester
Record Office: 10. Gerry Cranham: 11t, 36, 54t, 55, 56, 57,
86, 87t, 100, 102, 104, 106, 113, 114, 115, 120, 133t, 139t,
140, 141, 143t, 145, 157.E.T. Archive: 26, 31b, 34t, 79b, 130.
Mary Evans Picture Library: front cover, 18, 39, 42b, 46, 124.
William Hill Organisation: 79t, 82. Courtesy of Horse U.K.
Ltd.: 105, 108b, 109b. Kit Houghton: 11b, 107, 118, 133b,
142, 148, 149. Hulton Picture Company: 8, 12, 13t, 14, 15t,
16, 23, 25, 27, 42t, 44, 45, 62, 76, 128, 132, 162. Illustrated
London News: 61, 65b, 66, 67, 76, 77, 81t, 98t. Reproduced
by kind permission of the Jockey Club: 15b, 98b. Mansell
Collection: 28, 40. Trevor Meeks: 13b, 150, 151. Laurie
Morton: 9, 35, 158, 159, 160. Only Horses Picture Library:
81b, 161. Bernard Parkin: 38, 50b, 52b, 70, 89, 90, 134; 153/
Charles Parkin; 155b. Popperfoto: 48, 73, 84, 85bl, 85br,
108t, 109t, 112. Press Association: 17. W.W. Rouch & Co.:
125t. Dr. Jon Scargill: 59, 60. George Selwyn: 22, 51, 52t, 75,
87b, 88, 119, 124, 131, 143b, 146, 156. Courtesy of Peter
Smiles: 96. Sport & General: 85t, 94, 116, 117, 121, 138,
164. Sporting Pictures (U.K.) Ltd.: 21, 154. Syndication
International: 34b, 92, 139b. Bob Thomas Photography: 19,
47, 50t, 68t, 91, 111, 123, 144, 155t. Colin Wallace: 97.
Wolverhampton Borough Council: 171t. Courtesy of Wolverhampton Racecourse: 169, 171, 172.

Contents

Foreword by Peter Bromley   **6**

The Sport of Kings   How it all began   **7**

On the Toss of a Coin   The Derby   **14**

'Archer's Up!'   Fred Archer, 1857–86   **23**

Let the Buyer Beware   Tattersall's Sales   **29**

'Eclipse First, the Rest Nowhere'   Eclipse   **39**

A Good Place for a Picnic   Royal Ascot   **44**

Mantraps at Manton   The famous training establishment   **53**

Lucky To Be Alive   A trainer gets started   **58**

The 'Monkey on a Stick'   Tod Sloan, 1874–1933   **61**

The First Gentleman of Bookmaking   Archie Scott, 1904–65   **64**

Beating the Bookies   Alex Bird, professional punter   **71**

Sixty Years in Racing   Geoffrey Hamlyn, Starting Price reporter   **75**

'Arise, Sir Gordon'   Gordon Richards, 1904–86   **83**

Of Tradition, Triumph and Tragedy   Golden Miller and the Grand National   **86**

Keeping Up with the Chemist   Jockey Club Security   **96**

From Parachutes to Jumbo Jets   Racehorse transport through the ages   **104**

'The Man's a Genius'   Vincent O'Brien   **111**

The First Tuesday in November   The Melbourne Cup, Australia   **120**

The Legend   Lester Piggott   **127**

'Himself'   Arkle   **135**

'We're Amateurs!'   Point-to-pointing   **140**

Full Circle   Arab racing   **148**

'The Mare'   Dawn Run   **152**

Recruits for the Big Time   The British School of Racing   **157**

Running Commentary   Peter Bromley   **162**

'I Had a Tenner on!'   A Monday at Wolverhampton   **168**

Bibliography   **174**

Index   **175**

Foreword

by Peter Bromley

In writing a history of racing, embracing over two centuries and recording its important events and its notable personalities and horses, Anne Holland has faced up to a daunting task. She makes light of her work, dipping into the centuries in order to pursue her theme and constantly bringing the story right up to the present day. The early beginnings of racing in Britain are faithfully recorded and thanks to her meticulous research she is able to translate myths and legends into facts. The manner in which the names of the Derby and Oaks were decided on, by the toss of a coin, starts her examination of the great Epsom classics, and the Derby is brought up to date with a fulsome account of Kahyasi's win in 1988.

Jockeyship through the ages is dealt with in depth, starting with the romantic but sad tale of Fred Archer, whose career so closely resembled that of another tempestuous but brilliant jockey, Lester Piggott. Anne Holland quotes Fred Archer's grandson, John Tosetti, who reminds us that his grandfather had to ride his hack to reach the races, while today's jockeys have cars and helicopters. There is a vivid account of what has been described as Fred Archer's finest ride, his victory in the 1880 Derby on the Duke of Westminster's colt Bend Or: he won virtually one-handed after having had his arm savaged by a horse on Newmarket Heath.

There is a fascinating account, too, of the arrival of Tod Sloan from America: the impact that his crouching style had on jockeyship was enormous. At first he was called 'The Monkey on a Stick' and laughed out of court, but his skill at the starting barrier and his tactical sense soon started a new fashion. While Tod Sloan set the modern style of riding no jockey created such an indelible impression on all who watched him than Sir Gordon Richards. In the chapter 'Arise, Sir Gordon', Anne Holland does full justice to the man who epitomised all that is best in British racing. He was champion jockey 26 times and rode 200 winners or more on no less than 12 occasions. His death in 1986 at the age of eighty-two was a sad blow to racing; he is greatly missed.

Among other famous names who have played an important part in the development of racing in Europe is Vincent O'Brien, whose mastery at producing success-ful gambles at Cheltenham and Aintree was transferred to the preparation of flat-race horses of the highest class. Among his stars were Sir Ivor and Nijinsky.

The Grand National occupies a chapter. Like so many of us whose racing experience began only after the Second World War, Anne Holland is fascinated by the career of one of the greatest pre-war chasers, Golden Miller; and interwoven in the story is one of the most enigmatic characters in racing, his owner, the Hon. Dorothy Paget. I had not realised that 'The Miller' was ridden by a total of 17 different jockeys in his 52 races, of which he won 28.

Another 'Lady of Aintree' was Mirabel Topham, whose constant battles with the BBC over the copyright for the Grand National resulted in her mounting her own running commentary in 1952, which goes into the annals of history as one of the great broadcasting débâcles of all time.

Surely the greatest chaser of recent times was Arkle; his story makes nostalgic reading. At the height of his power and fame his career ended when he lamed himself after striking the take-off board of a fence at Kempton while competing in the King George VI Chase. Another great chaser whose career had a tragic end was Dawn Run. Anne Holland, who is also the author of the admirable biography *Dawn Run*, recounts her death at Auteuil and reminds us of one of the blackest days in National Hunt racing.

The growth of the bloodstock sales has been a twentieth century phenomenon. Tattersall's, the oldest sales company, began at Hyde Park Corner and in 1840 moved to Knightsbridge. Later they sold thoroughbred racing stock at Doncaster and Newmarket, before setting up at Newmarket only in the 1960s. The record price of 12,500 guineas established in 1872 stood for 24 years. The million-pound mark was passed in 1982 and the record now stands at 2.4 million for a colt sold at the Highflyer Sales in 1988.

Stride By Stride certainly covers the ground. It is a book that will be a necessity for racing professionals and connoisseurs, and yet I am sure it will be enjoyed just as much by those who know nothing of the origins of the sport. Anne Holland's research should whet their appetites, for racing is, in my experience, a sport that never loses its attraction once it grips you.

The Sport of Kings

How it all began

For as long as men have ridden horses they have laid wagers to determine whose is the best, be it in ancient times in the Middle East, or on the sands of New Zealand, straight off the ships importing them in the mid-nineteenth century; on the outskirts of the new Australian settlements from 1788, riding horses imported from England and South Africa, or along the newly hacked tracks of North America before any hinterland had been cleared. Or on the springy turfed expanses that made Newmarket Heath the natural headquarters of the racing industry. With good reason it is said that the United Kingdom comprises England, Scotland, Ireland, Wales – and Newmarket.

How courtiers must have moaned as they were forced to pack their bags and leave the comfort of Whitehall to take the jolty carriage drive towards the spartan offerings of Newmarket at Charles II's behest. Most of them had to camp at the foot of

Newmarket races, 1810, by Sartorius. '... jockies ... clap spurs to the willing horses, brandish their whips and cheer them with their cries.' (Henry II)

Warren Hill and carry out affairs of state from there, while the King, of course, had every luxury afforded him, right down to the secret passage from the Rutland Arms Hotel, across the road from his palace, whence Nell Gwyn used to visit him.

Charles II was a keen horseman and he loved racing: his Palace House Stables survived as a training establishment until the mid-1980s, but they now stand forlornly derelict, awaiting redevelopment. In 1665 he inaugurated the Newmarket Town Plate, declaring it should be run 'on the second Thursday in October for ever', a royal command that was obeyed until 1981, when the race was transferred to a Sunday. This move 'tested the water' regarding Sunday racing, and a crowd of about 3,000 was attracted, compared to the usual 200 or 300 on a Thursday; there were also two illegal bookmakers present.

Until 1972 the Town Plate, which still includes the famous Newmarket Sausages as part of its prize, was the only horse race in which women could compete under Jockey Club or National Hunt Rules. Yet horseracing was considered so important in the Arab world of the early centuries AD that 'even women were allowed to own racehorses'.

When war was declared in the Arab world over an alleged incident of foul riding in the sixth century AD, it took the intervention of the Prophet Mohammed himself several decades later to end it by drawing up rules of races, regulating ages of horses, size of fields and the distances. It was 1619

A view of Warren Hill in 1790, showing the running horses of noblemen, with grooms and horses in full livery, taking their exercise.

before formal rules covering rates, subscriptions, foul play and disqualifications were first introduced in England.

King Charles himself twice won the Plate, in 1671 and 1674, when, over three heats and a final, all of four miles on the round course, a chronicler of the time recorded 'the king wonn by good horsemanshipp'. Three centuries later, the future King Charles III, the current Prince of Wales, finished second in a charity two-mile Madhatters' flat race round the country National Hunt track of Plumpton below the South Downs.

Horseracing itself goes back to ancient times, when it flourished in Arabian countries. It was included in the Greek Olympiads, when money and sponsorship played a big part, although chariot racing was more popular. Records were kept from 776 BC until the abolition of the Games in AD 349, and women were strictly forbidden – all the male contestants were naked.

The Romans introduced racing to Britain, bringing Arab horses over with them, and the first recorded meeting was in about AD 210, at Netherby, Yorkshire, once the hub of the racing industry.

So although the three famous imports, the Byerley Turk, the Darley Arabian, and the

Godolphin Arabian, laid the foundation of the English Thoroughbred in the late seventeenth and early eighteenth centuries, their forebears had come to the country over a thousand years before. Racing in Roman Britain stood in such stead that those citizens of York who wished to improve their social status used to give cash to meetings, thus surely making them the sport's first sponsors in England, though they were way behind the Olympians.

In the ninth century 'running horses' were sent from France by one Hugh, founder of the Royal House of Capet, as a present to King Athelstan, whose sister Ethelswitha he 'was desirous of marrying'. Henry II described races at 'Smoothfield' (Smithfield) in which 'jockies inspired with thoughts of applause and in the hope of victory, clap spurs to the willing horses, brandish their whips and cheer them with their cries', a graphic early illustration of the thrill and glory with which the sport is inexorably linked, however much it has become scientific big business.

Edward III was presented with two running horses by the King of Navarre and just before his death, in 1377, his grandson, who was about to become Richard II, raced against the Earl of Arundel. Most races were matches and many of the horses were spoils of war.

This was certainly the case with the Byerley Turk three centuries later. Little could his rider, Captain Robert Byerley, have guessed the stud value of the horseflesh beneath him as he charged at the Battle of the Boyne, north of Dublin, in 1690! Byerley Turk's grandson, Partner, was the best racehorse of his day in 1718, as in turn was his grandson, Herod, in 1758. The mighty Herod's influence on the Thoroughbred is still felt.

The first fully established racecourse was founded during Henry VIII's reign, in 1540, on the

Palace House Stables, the oldest in Newmarket, formerly occupied by Charles II and extensively damaged by fire in April 1989.

Roodee, Chester. Laid out beside the city walls, the course is still full of character. Racing also became popular on the Knavesmire, outside the city walls of York, making a diversion for spectators from the regular hangings at the nearby Tyburn gallows. Frequent flooding from the River Ouse often made sport difficult; once, in the hard winter of 1607–8, racing actually took place on its frozen surface.

Towns all over the country ran race meetings and Tunbridge Wells was no exception, its course being on the Common around the ancient sand rocks. In 1799, when the town was losing its eminence to Brighton, a programme advertised:

> Diversions to be given by the Gentry visitants to promote Holyday Happiness in honour of the Brave Duke of York and the other officers and men employed in the Expedition against the Enemy who Means Good to Nobody; therefore Young and Old you may all come that will: play today and work on the Morrow but learn to be Merry and Wise.

An ass race was advertised as the second item on the programme:

> For a Cheshire cheese of a guinea value. Not less than six to start. The riders to have one spur and a whip . . . no stick or boots will be

Britain's oldest racecourse: the Roodee, set outside the city walls of Chester and almost circular, where racing has taken place since about 1540.

allowed, nor any Jockey that ever rode for £50. Silk or Satin Jackets the riders may wear. Entrance a Glass of Gin, at 10 o'clock, in the Queen's Grove, with Mr William Porter, Steward of the Course. To run according to the Plate Articles – Heats.

Another 'diversion' was for 'four men to smoke tobacco for a hat'!

It was James I who discovered the ideal hawking and coursing ground on the heath surrounding the New Market that was growing near Exning, between Cambridge and Mildenhall. There, on 8 March 1622, as an added diversion, Lord Salisbury and the Marquess of Buckingham matched their horses against each other for £100, and so began the racing life of a town whose whole being is geared to its two racecourses and the ancillary services.

Today, Newmarket boasts the finest studs in the land, including the National Stud, which has twelve separate yards. It had some 10,000 visitors in 1988, a figure expected to increase by 25 per cent in 1989. It houses the National Horseracing

Museum, which not only receives about 27,000 visitors per year but also conducts interesting and informative tours of the town, and there are research centres, bloodstock agents, auctioneers and transporters, a racing school, designers of all-weather tracks and top equestrian veterinary surgeons.

New yards, many on the American 'barn' style, are being built – some even with jacuzzis – and the equine population has doubled in half a century. Newmarket is thriving, thanks in no small measure to capital investment by the Arabs. About a third of the town's population is involved in one way or another in racing.

The National Stud, Newmarket, base for some of Britain's finest stallions and now open to the public.

Gallops stretch up Warren Hill, along the Limekilns reserved for major trials and pre-classic work; the all-weather Albahatri track has been joined by four more, enabling training to continue come rain, snow or frost. The training gallops are divided, by the town itself, between those on the

The Jockey Club owns most of the gallops in Newmarket, including the all-weather ones.

racecourse side and those on the Bury side. Most are owned and managed by the Jockey Club. The trees planted by prisoners of war on top of Warren Hill, a familiar landmark which provides shelter and a change of scene for horses to walk through, were mostly blown down in the gales of October 1987.

So James I really started something when he built a grandstand on the heath, improved the palace by adding new stables and, being out of luck with his own running horses, paid £154 in 1616 to a Master Markham for an Arabian horse. Charles I continued the racing tradition there when he was not 'otherwise engaged', and it was Charles II who made Newmarket really fashionable. The Rowley Mile, 'the finest straight mile', was named after his favourite hack, Old Rowley, and this also became the fun-loving king's own nickname.

From then on, down through the ages, racing was called the sport of kings: Queen Anne founded Ascot; one of George II's sons, the Duke of Cumberland, bred the two stallions which probably had the most influence on the modern Thorough-

bred, Herod and Eclipse; George IV was a great patron of the Turf and won the Derby in 1788, when he was Prince of Wales, with Sir Thomas; Queen Victoria, though not herself a racegoer, kept up the Royal Stud at Hampton Court; her son, later Edward VII, won no less than eight classics and a Grand National, including the 1896 and 1909 Derbies with Persimmon and Minoru, and his horse Diamond Jubilee is the only royal winner to date of the Triple Crown, in 1900, the year that Ambush II won the National; George V won one classic, the 1000 Guineas of 1928; and George VI, his son, won four of 1942's wartime substitute classics with Big Game and Sun Chariot.

Today, the sport of kings has a far broader base, with syndicate ownership enabling many ordinary people who could not afford their own horse to have a share in one. And company or corporate ownership has brought an 'image market'

Newmarket 1885. The Prince of Wales (centre front) is seen here with the Duchess of Manchester (left) and the Duchess of Montrose (right) whose name was linked romantically with Fred Archer (mounted).

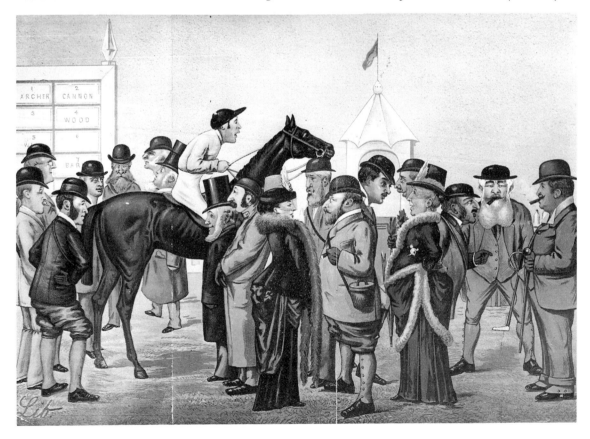

Hats off for a royal victory. Persimmon wins the Derby in 1896 for the Prince of Wales.

to the sport, with many clients barely moving from the hospitality tent to which they have been invited, their only glimpse of racing being on the television hung from the wall.

Yet there is still nothing the crowds and the grass-roots participants of racing today like more than to see a flat-race winner for the Queen, who has owned four horses who have won five classics, or a jumping one for the Queen Mother, whose Devon Loch was surely the unluckiest Grand National loser of all time; or to see the Princess Royal herself in action under either code, displaying the cool, calm courage that has brought her several wins both at home and abroad in a sport that truly sorts the 'men from the boys' and certainly gives no quarter to rank or calling in life.

The Princess Royal, seen here in action in 1989, continues the long tradition of royal involvement in racing.

On the Toss of a Coin

The Derby

June 1. Derby Day, 1988. For weeks now, the sporting press has been analysing the prospects. It is still the greatest, most prestigious horserace in the world, even if it is no longer the most valuable (that tag belongs to the Breeders' Cup in America in November). This year the Derby looks wide open; a fortnight ago, almost no top jockey had decided on his mount.

The one and a half miles of Epsom Downs provides the ultimate test of three-year-olds. They have to contend not only with the heightened atmosphere, tension, noise and excitement, but also with uphill and downhill gradients and the sweeping bend of Tattenham Corner.

There is no other atmosphere – or course – like it in the world. By ancient rights, the Downs are common land, open to all. And all, it seems, come on Derby Day: the gypsies, the fun fair, the hot-dog stands, the cockles, mussels and whelks stalls, the ice-cream sellers, the soothsayers, the pickpockets, the bookies, the tipsters, and the coachloads of trippers intent on enjoying their day out. For many of the nearly quarter of a million people attending, the reason for it all, the Derby, is a mere flash past of thunderous hooves – then it's the buzz as before.

The headaches for the organizers are enormous. No fewer than five roads cross the course. All have to be covered, four of them with coconut matting and one with wood chippings, to make them safe for the horses to cross. Because it is common land, there can be no permanent car parks and railings. The relatively new Walton, Tattenham and Lonsdale Enclosures are fenced in for the Derby meeting and a fence is erected around the caravan encampment.

Luckily, thanks to the unique Walton Downs Regulation Act of 1936, the racecourse itself, the grandstands complex and the training gallops are barred from the general public.

It was as a result of the chance discovery by a herdsman, Henry Wicker, in 1618 of water containing an unusual salt content with internal purgative qualities as well as external healing ones that Epsom became a fashionable health resort of the time, although it remained a small village for some years. Racing began at Epsom soon afterwards, as evidenced by a burial list of 1625 referring to 'William Stanley who in running the race fell from his horse and brake his neck'. Charles II is said to have watched, and by the time of Samuel Pepys, in 1663, the races there were famous enough to be included in his diary. By 1684 a clerk of the course, Devereux Watson, was employed, and from 1730 there were regular spring and autumn meetings.

In May 1769 the mighty Eclipse made his first racecourse appearance at Epsom. Ten years later Lord Derby, dining at his nearby home, The Oaks, with his friend Sir Charles Bunbury (racing's

The 12th Earl of Derby, 1752–1834.

Sir Charles Bunbury, 1740–1821.

staged at Doncaster the first major race to be decided on one running only, instead of heats, with the horses running just two miles instead of anything up to sixteen.

Thus was born the Oaks, for three-year-old fillies only, which was won by Lord Derby's own horse Bridget. Such was the success of the experiment that the following year the two men introduced another race for three-year-olds of either sex, colts to carry 8 stone and fillies 7 stone 11 pounds, over one mile. Legend has it that the name for the new race was determined by the toss of a coin – would it be the Derby Stakes or the Bunbury Stakes? In losing, Sir Charles gained swift and sweet recompense, for his horse Diomed won the inaugural running.

The Derby's first winner Diomed, who was owned by Sir Charles Bunbury and was unbeaten for his first three years' racing.

first 'dictator'), decided to let horses under four years old race, and over a shorter distance than the usual four or occasional two miles. They were following the trend set by Lieutenant-General Anthony St Leger, who three years earlier had

Racing at this time was still a fairly ribald, informal affair, but even so there were a number of conditions. One was that intended runners had to be at Epsom ten days before the start of the meeting, and fewer than three 'reputed running horses' would not constitute a proper start. They had to be stabled with subscribers in Epsom, who would subscribe 4 guineas or more towards the plates. Entry fees were 3 guineas per horse, 5s 'towards the repairs of ye rails' and 5s 'to ye Clerk of ye Course'; or, at the post, 6 guineas a horse, 5s for the rails and half a guinea for the clerk; and if an owner did not have his horse shod by a subscribing blacksmith in Epsom, he had to pay 2s 6d per horse.

For those who wanted to erect stalls or booths on the Downs, the cost increased the further away they lived: those from Epsom, 1 guinea; within twelve miles, 2 guineas; and any from further afield, 3 guineas per booth. If the fee was not paid on arrival, the booth would be destroyed, and, for good measure, they had to be put up in a straight line. The crowds swarmed into Epsom to watch and wager on the new spectacle, 'refreshed' by the Epsom waters or full of ale and carnival spirit, and figures topped 60,000 from its early years.

In Diomed, the Derby had a first winner worthy of the great race's reputation over 200 years later. The chestnut started 6–4 favourite and was ridden by Sam Arnull. Between them Sam, his brother John and C. Hindley were to ride eleven of the first twenty Derby winners.

Diomed's 1125-guinea win proved no fluke, for he remained unbeaten in his first three years' racing; but when he went to stud at six, having lost his form, he commanded a paltry 5 guineas' stud fee. Then, at the age of twenty, he was ignominiously sold by Bunbury for 50 guineas and shipped to the United States. There, he was sold to a Virginian breeder for 1000 guineas, but he proved his worth, for the old horse took on a

Carriages line the way and outriders precede the runners as Eager wins the Derby of 1791, portrayed by Sartorius.

new lease of life, becoming a leading American sire with a long line of winners to his credit.

The rest of that first Derby meeting consisted of a Noblemen's and Gentlemen's plate of £50, run in two four-mile heats on the first day; three four-mile heats for £50 on Derby Day; and a two-mile Ladies' Plate on Oaks day; the four-day meeting ended with heats for the four-mile Town Plate. There are those today who consider the supporting programme for the Derby and the Oaks just as boring and unenterprising, with the exception of the Coronation Cup.

The second- and third-placed horses in the first Derby were both by Eclipse, as was the following year's winner, Young Eclipse. He, like Sergeant in 1784 (the first year the Derby was run over one and a half miles), was owned by the now Colonel O'Kelly, owner of Eclipse.

In 1792 the great Frank Buckle won at odds-on on Patron, the first of five Derby successes from a total of sixteen classic wins. The 1804 winner, Hannibal, was ridden by William Arnull,

On Derby Day the Epsom Downs are traditionally a mass of stalls and booths of all descriptions. This was the scene in 1910.

nineteen-year-old son of Sam, and in this year the race was reported for the first time in *The Times*. There was a dead heat in 1828 and after a run-off the race went to Cadland; for the only other dead heat, in 1884, the prize was shared between St Gatien and Harvester.

In 1830, when the Derby celebrated its first half-century, Epsom could still be described as 'a large and remarkably pleasant village on the road from London to Dorking and Guildford'. There was a new stand and an above average winner in Priam, ridden for William Chifney by Sam Day, but, *The Times* reported, the races did not come off with their usual *éclat*. The fact that the twenty-one runners suffered fourteen false starts and a deluge during running might have had something to do with that observation.

GLOVES ETC.   THE FAVOURITE WINS   TIGHTLY WEDGED   MORE GLOVES.   HANGERS ON.   STRAIGHT FROM THE SHOULDER.   A VERY RESERVED SEAT.   PHIZ.   A WEL

OK MAKERS.   THE ARMY DRINKS.   HANG THE EXPENSE.   YOUNG ALLY SLOPER   ARABS NOT FROM THE EAST.   THE OLDEST VISITOR   BAD EGGS.   MUSIC HATH CHARMS ETC.   WEAL AND WOE.   LADIES IN WAITING.

Gypsies, a traditional part of the Epsom Downs scene on Derby Day, selling their 'lucky' heather.

How different today! Or is it? No one can prevent a deluge, or even a snow storm, and the advent of stalls does not automatically guarantee a perfect break, although it goes a long way towards doing so. The atmosphere hums every bit as much today as then; the Downs are embraced by the throng, increased from 60,000 to perhaps a quarter of a million, milling around the fun fair, stalls, and booths. For countless thousands of people, it is the day of the year, and on Derby Day, all roads lead to Epsom.

Naturally, traffic jams ensue, except for the growing number who arrive by helicopter, and 1988 was no exception. Thirty-four-year-old South African champion jockey, Michael Roberts, was keenly anticipating his first ride in the Derby on Maksud, trained by Robert Armstrong. But as he got within a few miles, his Mercedes ground to a halt and he was stuck, like everyone else, in the queue. The minutes ticked by. Roberts had his kit with him and, in desperation, waved down a passing motor-cyclist threading his way through the jam. Within moments, Roberts had abandoned his car and donned his crash hat, and the

cyclist obligingly took him pillion for the rest of the journey.

It was worse for Ian Balding, a trainer for the Queen, when in 1971 he too abandoned his car and ran the last two miles to the course in his top hat and tails. But since the marvellous Mill Reef won for him, such minor discomforts were readily forgotten.

But in 1932, the winning horse, April the Fifth, and his owner/trainer, Tom Walls, had to get out and walk after being stuck in a traffic jam.

Those who cannot get there at all, for whatever reason, can either listen on radio or watch on television, and in 1988 Radio 2's glamorous afternoon presenter Gloria Hunniford hosted the Derby programme, first broadcast on radio in 1927.

Nowadays the programme is more full of celebrities visiting Epsom and their chatter than serious race prospects. Star of screen and stage Liza Minnelli was enjoying her first visit 'enormously'. Footballer Mick Channon revealed he owns twenty-five to thirty horses himself, mostly brood mares and their offspring, plus about half a dozen in training. Actor Robert Powell was brought to the microphone between pauses for light music. And the effervescent Tommy Steele's enthusiasm bubbled through for all to share. Through him, the listening audience learned what it was like for a young Cockney kid to go to the Derby 'on the other side of the course' and to sample the whelks and hot dogs and gypsies and fun fair. This time, the great show biz star arrived by helicopter.

Only poor Peter Bromley was struggling to do a serious job on the day's first commentary race. 'I

OPPOSITE

Top An illustration by George Cruikshank showing not only the race but much of the behind-the-scenes activity. Among the colourful characters are 'a welsher', 'bookmakers' and 'ladies in waiting'.

Bottom The Epsom weighing room at the 1893 Derby. The race was won by Isinglass, considered by some to be the greatest racehorse ever.

can't see anything,' he bewailed, his normally calm, professional manner showing unusual signs of fraying. 'They've parked big green coaches right in front of the rails. All I can see are the jockeys' caps. I don't know how I'll be able to commentate, even for the Derby. They should do something about it, it shouldn't be allowed.'

Moments later, we heard they were off and running for the first race. The unflappable Peter had to make do with patter for one and a half furlongs, until the runners finally came into his view. Then he picked up smoothly and unflustered as Michael Roberts, justifying his unorthodox arrival at the course, beat the favourite, Sylvan Tempest, on the 25–1 outsider Sno Serenade for an all-the-way success.

Half an hour later, and he did it again in the Diomed Stakes, having to work considerably harder this time on the favourite, Waajib, to catch Luzum, whom the commentator had prematurely described as holding an unassailable lead.

What a sensational confidence booster for the eleven-times South African champion Michael as he prepared to partner Maksud, the third of Hamdan Al Maktoum's four runners in the Derby. The strong Arab influence, not least among names, has been felt since the late 1970s.

Next was the big one, sponsored since 1984 by Ever Ready, part of the Hanson Group. This time there was an hour between races. It was still a crush, as spectators tried to get a view of the fourteen runners. Most, it seemed, were still undecided about the likely winner if the headlines were anything to go by: Unfuwain, the 2000 Guineas winner, Doyoun, Red Glow, Charmer, Glacial Storm, Al Mufti, Sheriff's Star and Kahyasi all had their supporters.

Thinking that the television would give more serious coverage than radio, a switch to Channel 4 seemed called for – and up popped chirpy Tommy Steele again! To say nothing of the inevitable commercial breaks and Judith Chalmers paying far more attention to fashion than form.

The royal party walked along the course to the paddock, the Queen and the Princess Royal in glorious sunshine yellow outfits, the princess swirling a long umbrella; the Queen Mother was wearing one of her favourite blues that suit her so well.

At least we could see most of the horses in the paddock: Red Glow, living up to his name and looking a picture, proud and peacocky, trained for Eric Moller by Geoff Wragg and with Pat Eddery in the saddle; he seemed to justify favouritism. Unfuwain looked bigger and longer; his name, Radio 2 listeners were told, means 'pride and dignity' and he looked as though he could live up to it. He had American ace Steve Cauthen in the saddle.

A look at the race card revealed just how international the race has become: six of the horses had USA after their names; five were owned by Arabs and two by the Aga Khan; there was one Irish challenger, Project Manager, trained by Jim Bolger and ridden by the only apprentice in the race, twenty-one-year-old Kevin Manning; but none of the French entries had stood their ground.

The 100–1 chance, Clifton Chapel, trained by Steve Norton and ridden by Billy Newnes, was the only challenger from the north of England, an area which was once the most important in British racing. A horse from the north had not won a Derby since a war-time substitute at Newmarket forty-three years before, but Clifton Chapel's connections were hopeful of a place this time.

Royal trainer Dick Hern had three in the race, two for Lady Beaverbrook – Charmer, ridden by Paul Eddery, and Minster Son, ridden by his breeder, Willie Carson – as well as Unfuwain.

There was much housewives' support for the only lady-trained runner, who was also the only grey, Lady Anne Herries's Sheriff's Star, owned by her mother, Lavinia, Duchess of Norfolk, and ridden by Tony Ives. This was not the only family connection in the race: four of the jockeys were brothers, twins Michael Hills (Glacial Storm) and Richard Hills (Al Mufti, meaning 'person of high religious rank'); and Pat Eddery (Red Glow) and Paul Eddery (Charmer). Paul D'Arcy's mount, the pacemaker Al Muhalhal, was led round by his brother David, this horse and Al Mufti both being trained by Harry Thomson – 'Tom' – Jones.

Former Italian champion amateur rider Luca Cumani also trained two, Kefaah for Sheikh Al Maktoum, ridden by John Reid, and Kahyasi (named after a Turkish village), ridden by Ray Cochrane. Kahyasi was one of two runners for the Aga Khan, the other being the Michael Stoute-trained Doyoun; significantly, they were the only unbeaten colts in the race.

Doyoun, who pundits thought might have sta-

mina and temperament limitations, having only just lasted home in the 2000 Guineas, when he sweated up beforehand, had Michael Stoute himself at his head during the parade in front of the stands. Backers heaved their first sighs of relief as he appeared to remain cool and calm.

As the runners left behind their police escorts and headed off across the Downs for the start, there was another break for commercials on the TV coverage.

Interruption over and Sheriff's Star, attempting to become the first grey to win since Airborne in 1946 and only the fifth in all, had to be loaded first, having played up at the stalls on his last run. He tried it on again, but once in, stood as quiet as a lamb. The rest soon followed. Doyoun had remained calm and unruffled. One of the bright chestnuts had broken into a sweat. Within moments, the starter had them under way, and off they set up the hill, less steep since the start was altered 116 years ago but still testing.

Hamdan Al Maktoum's pair, Maksud and Al Muhalhal, struggled to reach the lead to pacemake, and soon his other two runners, Unfuwain and Al Mufti, were almost with them, each distinguished by a different coloured cap above the royal blue and white epaulettes of the silks. As they started the turn at the top of the hill, the favourite, Red Glow, was last of all.

Now they swung down towards the famous Tattenham Corner, where the unaccustomed camber would unbalance some, notably Charmer,

Kahyasi, owned by the Aga Khan, wins the 1988 Derby from Glacial Storm.

while Unfuwain, the only course and distance winner in the race, was unruffled by it. The grey Sheriff's Star ranged up towards the outside, but he was flat out and received a slap to keep him up to the task – which proved beyond him, as it was for Project Manager, another who tried hard.

Unfuwain maintained his lead and set sail for home; Kefaah looked to be going better than his stable companion, Kahyasi, at this stage, but the picture changed when it mattered. Two furlongs from home, with victory for Unfuwain still looking possible, suddenly there was Glacial Storm, and hot on his heels was Kahyasi, whose former hurdle-race jockey, Ray Cochrane, was completely unruffled in the hurly-burly of the world's premier race.

Red Glow, making belated headway, tried in vain to get a look in, while others, like the fancied stable companions Charmer and Minster Son, plus northern challenger, Clifton Chapel, barely caught the commentator's eye so much as once.

They were inside the final furlong – and Glacial Storm, tipped by several as a good each-way prospect, took over from Unfuwain; Doyoun was trying his hardest, but now neither could withstand the final spurt of Kahyasi. He ran on like the little cracker he is, beautifully partnered by Ray Cochrane. In the post-race euphoria, he

The Queen nearly always attends the Derby; here she is flanked by the Queen Mother and the Princess Royal.

A bird's-eye view of Kahyasi in the winner's enclosure.

revealed that he sought advice from the jailed maestro Lester Piggott on how best to ride the race.

So, it was the third Derby victory in eight years for the Aga Khan, following in the footsteps of his grandfather's five in twenty-two years between 1930 and 1952. He also won the St Leger five times and earned £1 million in prize money, making him the most successful owner at that time. The race time was a record since electrical timing started in 1964, but it remained four-hundredths of a second outside that held by the former Aga's Mahmoud in 1936.

The coffers of the current Aga, spiritual leader of the Ismaili Muslims, were swelled by £296,500 in prize money and Kahyasi, the eighth home-bred winner in the last eleven years, became worth a cool £10 million as a stallion.

The Derby has come a long way since Diomed earned 1125 guineas for Sir Charles Bunbury in 1780 and stood at stud for a fee of £5 per mare.

'Archer's Up!'

Fred Archer, 1857-86

Fred Archer's story is one of triumph and tragedy, love and sadness. Arguably the greatest jockey of all time, he commanded huge fees (much of which he passed on to his parents), was idolized yet had love for only one, and was modest and introspective off the course but ruthless and fired with burning ambition to win on it. At the height of his powers his beloved wife died. He was driven to distraction and compounded matters by purging his body to excess in order to ride in the Cambridgeshire at a low weight, making himself so ill that in a fit of delirium he shot himself. It was the ultimate tragedy, and it shook the whole racing world, from the highest in the land downwards.

During his greatness, men would greet each other in the streets with 'Archer's up', meaning all was well in the world. Inevitably, great jockeys, as great horses, are compared between one generation and another, in spite of changing times and circumstances. 'It is arrant nonsense to compare records because times have changed so much,' says John Tosetti, Fred Archer's grandson. 'My grandfather had to ride his hack to reach the races, whereas Gordon Richards would arrive in a chauffeur-driven Rolls, and today's jockeys have helicopters to wing them to two meetings in a day.'

Comparisons do, in fact, bear some scrutiny: Fred Archer, with the horse and rail transport available at the time, rode 2748 winners, including twenty-one classics, from 8084 rides, and was champion thirteen times in a seventeen-year career, an incredible one winner in every 2·9 rides; Gordon Richards, with the benefit of motor transport, rode 4870 winners, including fourteen classics, from 21,834 rides, and was champion an incredible twenty-six times in a thirty-four-year career, a ratio of one win in every 4·5 rides; Lester Piggott, with evening meetings and aircraft at his

Fred Archer in the fashionable attire of his day.

disposal, rode 4315 winners in Great Britain, including a record twenty-nine classics, from 19,552 rides and was champion eleven times in a thirty-seven-year career, a ratio of one win every 4·5 rides.

Like Lester Piggott, Fred Archer was born into racing, his father, William, having run away from his Cheltenham home to become a steeplechase jockey. At seventeen he was invited by Tsar Nicholas I of Russia to manage his stud and race his horses, which he did for two years, before the cold climate brought him back to England. A pugnacious little man, he was the right build for a jockey; the height which was to be the bane of his son Fred's racing life came from his tall, slender, good-looking mother, Emma Hayward.

Fred, their fourth child, was born in January 1857, and the following year his father won the Grand National on Little Charley. The family moved to nearby Prestbury, the village under Cleeve Hill, overlooking Cheltenham racecourse, which inspired another Prestbury resident, George Stevens, to become a steeplechase jockey. His five wins in the Grand National between 1856 and 1870 are still a record.

Fred Archer was nearly uneducated, not by choice but as a result of the influence of his father, who, rightly as it happened, prophesied that he would make more out of racing than anything else; this meant, though, that Fred could do little more than sign his name. Throughout his life, even at the height of his prowess, Fred lacked a certain amount of self-confidence and could be nervous and withdrawn once off his horse. But he was possessed by a demon on a horse, unrelenting with the whip and spurs and always alert at the start – which was especially crucial before the introduction of starting stalls. He was not averse to foul riding, stories of this being legion, but in those days it was barely frowned upon; only once in his career was he suspended, in 1871, following an altercation with the starter and another jockey, and he was stood down for a fortnight. He was totally analytical in his study of form books, as Lester Piggott was also to be. If he lost a race, he would go over and over it in his mind, often blaming himself when in truth he could have done no better. In fact, Fred Archer won numerous races that no other jockey on earth could have, but he never became big-headed and he commanded universal respect. The only jockey who could outwit him, to Fred's eternal exasperation, was George Fordham, who played 'cat and mouse' to great effect.

Fred Archer's race riding was legendary and by 1880, in his early twenties, he was earning £8000 a year, probably the equivalent of £200,000 today. This earned him his nickname, 'tin man', the slang for money. His daughter Molly received close on £½ million in his will, says John Tosetti. He also gambled heavily, as jockeys were allowed to in those days, but his honesty and will to win were such that even if it meant beating the horse his money was on, he did everything in his powers to come first.

He was only eleven when all thoughts of school were finally abandoned. His father had trained him long and hard on flighty ponies and was now quite convinced that his son had a natural riding genius (although some reports reckon nervous young Fred was more scared of his father than of either the ponies or the falls). So he found himself in Matt Dawson's Newmarket yard on trial, and there he stayed throughout his apprenticeship, treated as an equal with other lads at work but becoming more and more part of the Dawson family in private. At the age of twelve, Fred Archer had his first ride in public, in the Newmarket Town Plate at the second October meeting of 1869. His first win was a strange one, for it was on a pony in a steeplechase at Bangor later that year, when Archer weighed in at just 4 stone 11 pounds. In September 1870 he rode his first winner on the flat at Chesterfield; three years later, his apprenticeship over, Matt Dawson appointed him the stable's lightweight jockey and he finished second in the jockeys' table. In 1874, at the age of only seventeen and still able to ride at the minimum weight of 5 stone 7 pounds, he became champion jockey with 147 wins. He was to remain at the head of the leader table for the rest of his life. It was also the time when he shot up in height and consequently weight. Matt Dawson consulted with his principal owner Lord Falmouth, for whom Archer was to ride twelve classic winners, and appointed him overall stable jockey. Fred Archer went from having to carry upwards of three stone of dead weight under his saddle to having to diet strictly, inventing 'Archer's mixture', a devastating purgative. For breakfast he would have a tablespoon of hot castor oil and half an orange; lunch consisted of a sardine and a small glass of champagne; and he spent much of his time in a Turkish bath. In his all too brief seventeen-year career, Fred Archer was champion jockey thirteen times. He would leave his Newmarket home to ride thirteen miles to Cambridge

Fred Archer in racing silks, before helmets were compulsory beneath caps.

station to catch the train to whichever race meeting he was attending.

It was Fred Archer's deserved good fortune that he rode two of the best horses in the history of horseracing, St Simon and Ormonde, although he was not engaged exclusively for either. St Simon was unbeaten in his nine races, and although he did not run in any classics, Matt Dawson considered him the best horse he ever trained. By a Derby winner, Galopin, he was desperately highly strung and once bolted with Fred on Newmarket Heath; Fred was replaced as his jockey, which may have been rather harsh treatment, but it did not stop the horse winning and, in spite of his temperament, he went on to be an outstanding sire, heading the champion sire list nine times.

Occasionally racing goes through peak periods, and the late nineteenth century was well and truly a golden age. Only two years after the birth of

St Simon, Ormonde came along. He too was unbeaten, and won the Triple Crown as well. Also by a Derby winner, Bend Or, he was trained by John Porter at Kingsclere for the 1st Duke of Westminster. The 2000 Guineas of 1886 was probably the best of all time: The Bard had won all sixteen of his races as a two-year-old; Saraband and the favourite, Minting, had much to recommend them, and Ormonde had won his only three races in the autumn of his two-year-old career. Ormonde won as he liked and Fred Archer, who rode Minting, ensured he was on Ormonde for the Derby. He won the St Leger at odds of 7–1 on, the Great Foal Stakes at Newmarket at 25–1 on, and the Champion Stakes at 100–1 on!

One of Fred Archer's greatest feats of horsemanship was in the Derby of 1880, which is generally considered to be his finest race. He won virtually one-handed on Bend Or, having had his arm savaged by Muley Edris on Newmarket Heath. The colt, it seems, had not forgotten thrashings Fred had given it in races, and when Fred dismounted to lead him home after work, Muley Edris literally set about him and bit his arm so severely that at one time it seemed as if it might have to be amputated. But, a bit like Lester Piggott when his ear was torn off, Archer refused to let the injury interfere with the business of riding classic winners, although as Derby Day approached and his arm was no nearer healing, he became very depressed. He declared himself fit, and rode, but looked like losing the race to Robert the Devil; he gave away the inside to no one, coming so close on the rails round Tattenham Corner that he had to lift his left leg, but Robert the Devil had first run; Bend Or, plagued by sore shins, was unbalanced and victory looked a forlorn hope, all the more so when Fred, automatically going for his whip with his useless arm, dropped it. But Robert the Devil's rider made the fatal error of looking round; Fred grabbed his chance and with almost supernatural strength lifted Bend Or to victory by the shortest of margins.

Fred Archer was on a crest; he won both the Derby and the St Leger on Iroquois, the first American-bred horse to do so – the consternation of British racegoers was allayed only by the fact that Fred was riding; he won the City and Suburban, the Epsom Gold Cup and the Champion Stakes on Bend Or (who went on to become an

25

Fred Archer on Ormonde, the 1st Duke of Westminster's unbeaten winner. In 1886 Ormonde won the prestigious Triple Crown.

influential sire); and his total wins were 220. He then dashed many ardent girls' dreams by falling in love with Helen Rose Dawson, daughter of Matt's brother.

The couple were married in January 1883, after Fred had had a magnificent, typically Victorian mansion built with no expense spared; special trains were laid on to bring in well-wishers from the surrounding countryside and the streets of Newmarket were lined with cheering crowds. The house, named after Lord Falmouth, was filled with wedding presents from all around the country, from the highest-ranking downwards, with racing trophies and portraits. Fred Archer worshipped his pretty young wife and was besotted by her. A year later, she gave birth to a son who lived for only a few hours; Helen herself lay at death's door for several weeks. Fred spent every waking hour that he was not racing by her side until she recovered. Less than a year later, she gave birth to their daughter, but this time she did not recover.

Her death was a devastating blow, and one from which Fred Archer literally never recovered. A break that winter in America, instead of following his usual winter pursuit of hunting, eased the burden a little, or rather, took his mind off it, but when he came back he threw himself into the only thing he really knew, racing. He rode the staggering total of 246 winners in that one season. It was as if an inner jet propelled him ever on, but nothing could compensate for his personal loss.

The following season, with Matt Dawson retired, Lord Falmouth's string cut to almost none (it was on one of his few remaining horses, Blanchard, that Fred rode what turned out to be his last winner) and rumours of chicanery circulating about Archer, ever the man with the greatest

integrity, all proved too much. He was determined to ride the winner of the Cambridgeshire for the Duchess of Montrose, almost certainly the only woman who could be linked romantically with him with any justification, in spite of her more senior years. It is said she proposed to him but that he pointed out to a close friend, 'I don't think I had better do it, do you? And, anyhow, it would not make me a duke!'

The horse he was to ride for her was St Mirren, but to do so he had to lose what was even for him an abnormal amount of weight. He lost the race (by a head), a lot of money and a lot of face. Despite his dejection, he travelled to Brighton, where two winnerless days brought even more depression. The South Downs are cold and windy at the best of times, and this was November, but he continued on to Lewes, when he should have been home, and was beaten out of sight on the odds-on favourite, Tommy Tittlemouse.

He was escorted home by train in a fever, and the chill turned into typhoid. News of his illness spread quickly and soon his house, where his sister, Mrs Coleman, now resided and looked after his daughter, was filled with get-well messages; two physicians were in attendance and soon proclaimed him on the mend, but yet again that devil depression got the better of him. He was sure he was going to die and after a few days, quite out of his mind, he grabbed the gun kept to guard the fine possessions in the house from burglars and shot himself. His poor sister struggled to wrest the gun from him, but it was too late. His death was the ultimate tragedy in racing.

His orphan daughter, Nelly Rose, was brought

Bend Or, ridden by Fred Archer, wins the 1881 Gold Cup at Epsom by a neck from Robert the Devil.

Fred Archer looking gaunt and thin at what was his last appearance at Newmarket.

up by the Dawsons, chiefly by Matt's daughter Annie in Newmarket and then in Marlow, Buckinghamshire, and in 1911 she married Max Tosetti, whose father had moved from Como to England, where Max was born. They had three daughters, who now live in Spain, Australia and Cornwall, and one son, John.

The family grew up in a lovely home in mid-Sussex, from where Nelly Rose pursued her interest in racing by attending meetings regularly, and she often went out in a pony and trap. Her son, John, was only fourteen when she died, but the racing connection continued a little longer, as he rode in a few point-to-points and steeplechases. From school in Uppingham he continued the

family association with the Dawsons, who used to take him out for weekends to their home in Newmarket. Imagine John's surprise when he was called up in the last war, kitted out in Norwich and sent off in a train, destination unknown, to find himself marching up Newmarket High Street to be billeted in Heath House, where Fred Archer was apprenticed! It looks as if the racing bug has finally died out from the family as none of John's children or those of his sisters show the slightest inclination towards racing. But the legend of Fred Archer will never die, and there are those in Newmarket today who swear his ghost rides down Hamilton Road every morning still.

Let the Buyer Beware

Tattersall's Sales

An expectant hush settles over Park Paddocks, Newmarket. Elegant lights shine on the covered ring surrounded by tiers of padded seats. Outside, the lines of parked cars slope away from the stone arch that was transported from London in 1956 to dominate the entrance; lawns are beautifully mown and surrounded by brightly coloured beds of dahlias and one or two fountains. The 750 stables stretch out in different yards behind, covering forty-two acres.

It is early evening and trainers, owners and agents from all quarters of the racing globe turn their eyes towards the yearling being led in. The auctioneer, in regulation tweed jacket, reads out the catalogue details of the bay colt by Northern Dancer out of Fairy Bridge (USA). He is small and active, the only white on his lithe body a bold star on his forehead. The bidding turns into yet another duel between Robert Sangster's representative, on this occasion James Delahooke, and the Maktoum brothers. It reaches 1 million guineas; it passes the 1·55 million British record; at 2·4 million guineas, Sheikh Mohammed bows out, one bid short of establishing a European record, and the yearling will join Vincent O'Brien's stable, from whose stud the colt was offered. It is the Highflyer Sales, run by Tattersall's in late September. They are England's most historic auction house, their story as steeped in racing as any of the humans and horses attending. The 389 yearlings on offer over the four days have each been individually inspected by Messrs Tattersall's staff in the preceding five months, in England, Ireland, France and America, and only those considered the best on both breeding and conformation are selected for this sale; the remainder are booked for the October Sales.

Gone are the days when long-established studs could monopolize the prime places in the sales; now there is a rigorously adhered to rota worked out by Tattersall's to give all breeders an equal chance of a good place in a sale. The electronic number board, modernized again since the last one got stuck on 999,990 when the million-pound barrier was broken for the first time, in 1982, shows the prices not only in pounds but also in dollars, yen, French francs and lire. As the bidding starts in earnest, the video lens zooms in discreetly on the bidders, a necessity since the notorious 'Lot 116' case of 1983, when the purchaser reneged on his obligation.

It all seems a far cry from the day in 1776 when Richard Tattersall founded the firm – in the same year that the fine art auction house of Christie's also came into being – and yet much has stayed the same. It remains a business for those inexorably bound up in horseracing, as was the case with generations of Tattersalls and is with today's chairman, Michael Watt, himself a descendant of Lord George Bentinck, the second of racing's famous first three 'dictators'.

Richard Tattersall himself was a Lancashire lad who hid his first pony in a barn and exercised it at dawn after buying it secretly to escape his father's wrath; it was no surprise that he went to London to seek his fortune, married well and, after attending many of the then numerous auction sales, determined to succeed in the business himself.

His enterprise and connection in high places enabled him to rent some fields near Hyde Park Corner from the Earl of Grosvenor on a ninety-nine-year lease, near where the old St George's Hospital building stands, towards the new Berkeley Hotel. In those days it was bounded by the Bloody Bridge, a plank across the Westbourne, south of where Sloane Square is now; it was the haunt of robbers and murderers who would trap travellers as they tried to cross over it, so Richard sited his repository at the end further away, near the Turf Tavern.

Richard Tattersall with Highflyer in the background.

Three years later he managed to buy the un-beaten colt Highflyer, and sent him to stud on his farm near Ely, mating him with as many daughters of Eclipse as he could lay his hands on to found an influential line. It is after this appro-priately named horse that the firm's chief sales are called today.

Ponies, hacks, hunters, racehorses, hounds and carriages were all sold in Richard Tattersall's day, in contrast to just Thoroughbreds now, but much of the actual method of auctioneering and the conditions of sale have remained the same for over 200 years.

When Tattersall died, one of his executors was James Weatherby, whose family has been tied up in racing for just as long as the Tattersalls. The firm Weatherby's came into being in 1773: James was first Keeper of the Match Book to the Jockey Club from 1777 and another Mr Weatherby from the same family started the General Stud Book in 1791. The natural progression was for Weatherby's to become secretaries to the Jockey Club, seeing to the day-to-day administrative side of racing, and becoming in effect the Jockey Club's civil service ever since. It was only in the 1980s that for the first time – following the death of Simon Weatherby – a member of the Weatherby family was not secretary to the Jockey Club. However, the chairman is Christopher Weatherby.

It is from Tattersall's that both racecourse enclosures and the betting disciplinary committee take their name. It became the practice among gentlemen in London in those early days to dine at Tattersall's repository, first at its Hyde Park Corner premises and later at Knightsbridge, when the lease ran out. Here they struck and settled wagers on the racing, and it then became the custom to meet on Mondays to settle any out-standing wagers or disputes relating to them.

Tattersall's Committee was founded in 1795 and in 1843 the second Richard Tattersall (who bought the St Leger winner The Colonel when he conducted the dispersal sale of the Royal Stud at Hampton Court after the accession of Queen Victoria) published new rules and regulations concerning the Subscription Rooms. A year later, when the Jockey Club was trying to free itself from the responsibility of settling betting dis-putes, he gave evidence to a Special Committee on the Gaming Laws presided over by Lord Palmerston.

During this, he said racing could not survive if betting was not legalized, and added that the advent of railways had caused a general fall in the prices of horses. The expense of transporting racehorses by van, pulled by four horses, had increased greatly and rail costs were very high. It was desirable not only to legalize betting, he said, but to give power of recouping dishonoured bets to a court of law. It was agreed that for an annual subscription of two guineas, his Rooms could be entered every Monday and Thursday, in effect legalizing credit betting among the gentry. Bet-ting on the streets remained illegal until 1961, when the first betting shops opened.

By the time Tattersall's lease ran out on the Hyde Park Corner site in 1865, it was a well-established force in eminent breeding and racing circles. In 1837, Lord George Bentinck had bought a twenty-two-year-old mare with filly foal at foot for 54 guineas; the foal was called Crucifix and not

A horse for sale is run up to show off its paces to prospective purchasers, a practice which continues today.

Sceptre, sold at Tattersall's in 1900, won four classics in 1902 and was considered unlucky not to have become the only horse ever to win all five.

only won the 1000 and 2000 Guineas and the Oaks, but was dam of the Derby winner Surplice too.

The move to Knightsbridge in the late nineteenth century, while it was still the haunt of footpads and thieves, was to last until 1939, and the buildings continued in use for administrative purposes until 1977. Sales were also conducted at various studs over the country, and at Doncaster and Newmarket, and it was not until the 1960s that they finally settled on Newmarket alone. From 1870 the July Sales were held in the open air outside the Salutation Inn in Newmarket. In 1884 Edmund Somerville – 'Sommy' – Tattersall, who was to steer the firm during its most crucial period and was sadly the last of the Tattersalls when he died in 1942, built a ring with seating and rostrum, offices and a small refreshment room which continued in use for the firm's guests until 1940.

The year 1900 saw not only a new century but

The first sale at Tattersall's new buildings. This sketch of gentlemen sizing up the best horses appeared in the Illustrated London News *in 1865.*

also record prices, a far rarer occurrence then than now; it was at the dispersal sale of the Duke of Westminster at Kingsclere that the Triple Crown winner Flying Fox was sold for 37,500 guineas, a record for a horse in training that was to stand for sixty-seven years – and was then broken by nearly 100,000 guineas when the two-year-old Vaguely Noble fetched 136,000 guineas!

Even more dramatic, perhaps, was the sale of the 'Flying Filly', Sceptre. Robert Sievier, who had already made his name as (to quote Peter Willett) 'a soldier, actor, owner, professional backer, journalist and charlatan', was determined to acquire the yearling by Persimmon out of Ornament. The trainer John Porter was equally set on her. To 'Sommy's' consternation, Sievier thrust £20,000 in banknotes into his hands the night before as a deposit. Since the yearling record at that time was 6000 guineas, he was naturally worried at being responsible for so much

money; he hid it on top of the wardrobe in the Rutland Arms Hotel, where he was staying, and rushed it to the bank as soon as it was open in the morning.

At the sale itself, after spirited bidding between the two chief rivals, Sievier purchased the filly for the record 10,000 guineas. It proved a shrewd move, for she was one of the greatest horses of all time, and almost certainly unlucky not to become the only horse ever to win the Grand Slam of all five classics; indeed, had John Porter succeeded in his bid for her, she might now be in the record books, for by all accounts in his hands she would certainly have been more sympathetically handled.

There were several record yearling prices after

the First World War, until sales dropped in the 1920s; one of the strongest buyers of the period was the Aga Khan, who as an owner was to win over fifty European classics, including the Triple Crown (2000 Guineas, Derby and St Leger) with Bahram and the Derby with Mahmoud. He was leading owner thirteen times. The spiritual head of Ismaili Muslims, he was very popular, and racing has continued in the family in spite of many other responsibilities and interests. His grandson, the present Aga Khan, won the Derby in 1981, 1986 and 1988 with Shergar, Shahrastani and Kahyasi.

It was also between the wars that the training establishment at Manton was sold, on condition that its incumbent, the brilliant but part recluse Alec Taylor, could train there until he retired. Waldorf Astor had horses there, and Gerald Deane of Tattersall's was employed by him in an advisory capacity. When Taylor retired, the firm of Tattersall's bought Manton, thus furthering their interest in racing first hand, and employed head lad Joe Lawson as trainer, with considerable success.

It was between the wars that the more commercial type of breeder began to appear, and six future Derby winners were sold by Tattersall's as yearlings at either Doncaster or Newmarket. After the Second World War a new breed of owner began to emerge, starting with radio and television rentals magnate David Robinson. His policy was quantity rather than quality, going for the precocious two-year-old who was likely to offer a quick return on his investment, and he was a big spender in the late 1960s and early 1970s. Soon after that, Robinson's methods were adapted, developed and refined on an international scale by the Robert Sangster/Vincent O'Brien team with enormous success, going far more for the potential classic winner and future stallion. It was the beginning of the bloodstock explosion, only to be halted in its tracks by the effects of the Gulf War in 1973, when crude oil prices quadrupled and inflation hit the Western World.

It was also a time of adaptation and modernization in auctioneering, with sales becoming split between foals and yearlings one week and fillies, brood mares and horses in training the next, instead of being all jumbled up together.

It was in the late 1970s that the bloodstock

explosion finally burst, and it is interesting to see just how dramatic it was: in 1872, the record stood at 12,500 guineas, and twenty-four years later it went up by just 2000 guineas; then came Flying Fox in 1900 at 37,500, followed thirty-two years later by the stallion Solario, who made 47,000. The first huge jump came with Vaguely Noble's 136,000 in 1967, but it was in the 1970s that records tumbled about all over the place: 1975 saw a filly yearling by Mill Reef make 202,000; in 1977 a Lyphard yearling fetched 250,000; and a year later the three-year-old filly Swiss Maid was sold for 325,000; the year after that saw another Lyphard yearling, sold this time for 625,000. A brood mare made 730,000 in 1981; the million-pound barrier was broken in 1982, when a three-year-old filly, Tenea, made 1,020,000, a record broken yet again only one year later when a yearling colt by Hello Gorgeous made 1,550,000. That record stood for six years, until the 2.4 million colt at the 1988 Highflyer Sales, when two colts by Nijinsky also topped one million.

An offshoot of the enormous rise in oil prices in the early 1970s was that a number of oil-rich Arab states suddenly found themselves phenomenally wealthy; and, to the great benefit of British racing, a good many of their leading families vested their racing interests here. England has the greatest racing history and tradition; the sport is run superbly under the jurisdiction of the Jockey Club (even if outdated in some respects, their administration of racing leaves authorities in some other sports trailing miles behind); and England had many links with the Arabs in the past, going right back to the foundation of Thoroughbred racehorses themselves through Arab horse influence.

So their impression on British racing has been entirely appropriate and has in almost all circles been warmly welcomed. Michael Watt says:

After the war, Americans could buy any good brood mare, filly and most of the stallions; they had tremendous tax advantages because they could run the horse two or three times and then claim the whole purchase price back when it went to stud.

The Arabs redressed the balance between old and new; they brought horses back from Kentucky to here.

He added further praise, as have many others, by saying, 'The Arabs are so sporting, they like to

33

Above *Flying Fox, winner of the 1899 Triple Crown, was sold at Tattersall's in 1900 for the then record price of 37,500 guineas.*

Below *1967 saw the first huge leap in bloodstock prices when Vaguely Noble, pictured here before the sale, fetched 136,000 guineas.*

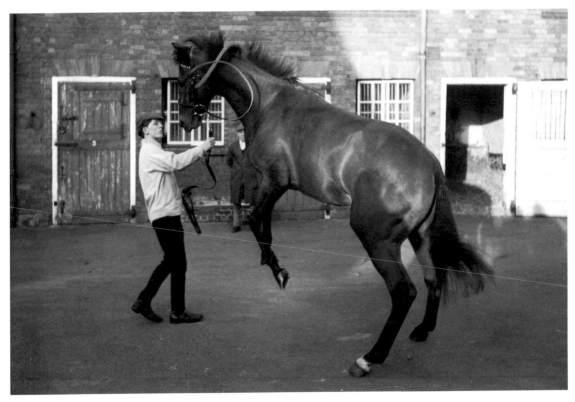

Michael Watt, Chairman of Tattersall's. All his auctioneers undergo RADA training before taking up positions.

win and have the best but they are very good in defeat.'

The only rumblings of resentment have been from small-time owners and trainers who say they cannot even win at little meetings when Arab-owned horses turn up there; but conversely, when Arabs offload their less good horses, they are usually plenty good enough for English people who would not otherwise have had the chance to buy. Several Arabs have set up studs in England and Ireland, as well as in America and Australia.

In Michael Watt, the family tradition of Tattersall's is continuing; his father, Terence, was made a partner in the war but was killed flying; his cousin Ken came in, and was chairman until Michael succeeded him in 1982. Michael joined in 1954 (the same year as Gerald Deane's son Bruce), after Eton and the Life Guards, but not until he had spent a year enjoying his favourite pastime, hunting. The firm was getting over the difficulties of the war years, and the socialist restrictions after it, thanks to the determination of Kenneth Watt following the untimely deaths of his partners, Gerald Deane and Robert Needham.

A major sale soon after Michael joined was the dispersal of the late Mr Dewar's horses at the December Sales, resulting in a turnover of a million pounds for the first time; now turnover is about £88 million a year.

A new restaurant was built; previously the only eating place for visitors from all over the world was a straw-filled tent with benches. The little wooden sales ring was too small and outmoded too, and expansion was as imperative as modernization. Sir Albert Richardson, president of the Royal Academy, was called in to design the impressive new set-up that has since become the focal point for racing people the world over.

The bidding heats up, the auctioneer coaxes and cajoles, leaning forward over the rostrum, gavel in hand, his ever-alert eyes spotting the discreet bidders. It is no accident that spectators can clearly hear every word he says, however fast he speaks, or that the whole affair smacks of the theatrical, for these auctioneers are showmen playing to their audience, intent on keeping their attention and interest. It is no spurious analogy to compare auctioneering with acting – all the Tattersall's auctioneers have attended voice training at the Royal Academy of Dramatic Art, Britain's best-known theatre school.

With nine auctioneers, Tattersall's has more than most European and American auctions, and their style is different too. The English idea is to change auctioneers regularly to keep freshness in front of the public, each having his individual style. In America, the whole thing is more formal: the auctioneers wear dinner jackets and their speech is more of a chant; much of the 'spotting' is done by glamorous girls dressed in uniform and they can even take bids themselves. There, the horse being sold stands still in the middle of the ring, whereas in England and Ireland they walk around. 'We are not averse to moving with the times,' says Michael Watt, 'but with a horse walking round, the public can see his action.'

In 1988, Tattersall's opened their new auction house in Ireland, in a lavish purpose-built complex near Fairyhouse Racecourse, replacing the cramped conditions at Ballsbridge. Here more emphasis is put on National Hunt produce.

Over the centuries, Tattersall's have resisted pressure to sell their horses warranted sound, relying instead on the time-honoured tradition of *Caveat emptor* – Let the buyer beware. Nevertheless, every yearling they accept has first been tested in its wind; as for the rest, it is up to buyers to satisfy themselves, by watching the horse's action, noting its conformation and any blemishes, and there is nothing to prevent buyers or their vets sounding the horse's heart with a stethoscope before it enters the ring.

The 'Lot 116' case was a different matter. From time immemorial, auctioneering has relied greatly on gentlemanly conduct and although there are all types in the racing world, this has worked almost

A picture illustrating all the features of the modern sales ring, at Newmarket, the headquarters of British racing.

Deep in thought . . . Buying yearlings is a serious business.

infallibly. When there is a dispute, usually when two bidders both believe they have secured the purchase, the lot is immediately reoffered; but in this case, the purchaser denied he had had the final bid at all and refused to sign the purchase slip.

The next lot was already in the ring, and this was the one everyone was expectantly awaiting, the Hello Gorgeous colt, who made the record 1,550,000 guineas. After that, much of the evening's interest waned, and with several more lots sold by the time the purchaser of Lot 116 had been spoken to, immediate resale was impossible. To put the horse up again at the end of the evening, when many prospective buyers would have left, was considered detrimental to the vendors' interests.

The man who made the final bid promised to return in ten minutes, but he never reappeared. So Tattersall's contacted the underbidders; they, however, wanted nothing further to do with it, and the colt was resold two days later for half the sum it had fetched originally, although still £50,000 more than the reserve sum the vendors had put on it.

Dissatisfied, they sued Tattersall's for negligence, saying the colt should have been resold the same night. Twenty months later, the case reached the High Court, lasted for thirteen days, with the judge deliberating a further four, and resulted in Tattersall's being fully vindicated. It was a case with great significance not just for bloodstock but for fine art and other important auction houses too, and would have meant the altering of many auctioneering traditions in order to safeguard themselves had it gone against them.

Ironically, Lot 116 won three class races in Germany and two in England, whereas the record-breaking Lot 117 ran unplaced twice in Ireland as a two-year-old.

It is this very uncertainty, of course, on which sales thrive. As Michael Watt says, 'If breeding was an exact science and the results a foregone conclusion, Tattersall's would have gone broke years ago: the top colt would make ten million and the rest nothing.'

As it is, sales such as those in Newmarket, Ireland, Keeneland in Kentucky and so forth act both as a nerve centre of the modern racing industry and an exclusive type of club, one to which, nevertheless, anyone can come.

Part and parcel of modern racing is sponsorship, and yet it is not really an innovation. Tattersall's, for instance, first sponsored a race in 1849 over the Rowley Mile at Newmarket. The practice was not repeated until over thirty years later, when in 1880 the Somerville Stakes, for two-year-olds that had been sold by Tattersall's, was run at the Newmarket second spring meeting, with £300 put up by the Jockey Club and £200 by Tattersall's. In 1899, the Jockey Club dropped its contribution but the race continued, sponsored by the auctioneers, and was renamed the Somerville Tattersall Stakes in 1958.

By 1986, Tattersall's sponsored two group 1

The Highflyer Sales, Newmarket. The Vincent O'Brien team from Coolmore is seen here inspecting a yearling before the sales.

two-year-old races in England, the Cheveley Park and Middle Park Stakes, and the group 3 Musidora Stakes, as well as a group 2 and group 3 race in Ireland. Not forgetting the National Hunt side, they began the Tattersall's Mares Only Novice Chase series in 1983, and by 1986 their total annual sponsorship amounted to £192,750.

Racing is a sport and industry in which people from all walks of life become totally bound up, and someone like Michael Watt cannot bear the thought of retiring. But with a cousin, Richard Mildmay-White, waiting in the wings, he is safe in the knowledge that the old firm will maintain its long family tradition.

'Eclipse First, the Rest Nowhere'

Eclipse

It was dark as night that late March day in 1764 when William Duke of Cumberland's unraced mare Spiletta gave birth to a chestnut colt with one white leg by Markse. He named the foal Eclipse, but sadly did not live to see him mature; on the duke's death, the young colt became just another lot number at his dispersal sale at Windsor Forest.

He was rather large and ugly as a yearling and there was no reason to suppose there would be much interest in him; but one William Wildman, a butcher 'of much prosperity' from Smithfield, had set his heart on him. So imagine his disappointment when he arrived at the sale to find

The mighty Eclipse, with his glossy chestnut coat and famous white leg.

the lot already put up and sold for 70 guineas. He looked at his watch, discovered the sale had been started before the advertised time – and insisted on all sold lots being reoffered. This time he secured his intended purchase, paying either 75 or 80 guineas according to different records. He soon found he had a somewhat intransigent yearling on his hands; not so much bad-tempered as high-spirited and capricious. William Wilding sent him to a nagsman at Epsom to be broken in and sorted out, where he was 'ridden all day and occasionally all night as well', but nothing broke his spirit. The horse seemed prepared to go on for ever.

The wonder of it all is that Eclipse was not gelded as a way of curbing his exuberances, though his connections must have been sorely tempted to do so. From the outset he possessed that prime, intangible quality in a racehorse, 'heart', the will to win. Perhaps it is no coinci-

William Duke of Cumberland, 1721–65, Eclipse's first owner.

dence that on his death his heart was found to weigh 14 pounds.

William Wildman was nothing if not patient, and to his eternal credit, he waited until Eclipse was five years old before considering racing him, which was the more usual age in those days. First, he gave him a pre-dawn trial at Epsom against a proven older horse. They succeeded in completing the trial before the inevitable 'spies' were out, although the touts managed to collar an old woman who had been on the downs since day break. 'Yes,' she said, she had seen a horse with a white leg 'running away at a monstrous rate', the other so far behind that she was sure it would never catch up 'even if he ran to the world's end'!

There have been 'talking horses' since time immemorial, but Eclipse indeed proved to be that 'something else'. So it was at Epsom in 1769 that Eclipse made his racecourse debut, starting at odds of 4–1 on for a prize of 50 guineas against Gower, Cade, Trial and Plume, in heats of four miles. Eclipse, ridden by John Oakley, won the first heat so impressively that an Irish onlooker, one Major Dennis O'Kelly, wagered that he would correctly place all the runners in the second. His bet, which has become a part of racing lore, was: Eclipse first, the rest nowhere. That is, all the others would be beaten by a 'distance' (240 yards), so that the judge would not officially place them.

After the customary thirty minutes' rubbing down, Eclipse and his opponents cantered back the four miles to the start of the course, where they were again called into line and sent on their way. For the first three miles, Eclipse stayed with his opponents, but then he drew right away and duly won by a distance, which also meant he won the race outright without the need for another heat. What's more, O'Kelly had put his money where his mouth was by there and then purchasing a half share in the horse for 650 guineas. The following year, he paid another 1000 guineas in order to buy him outright.

It was the same story for Eclipse's second race at Ascot, when he earned another 50 guineas by beating Cream de Bauble. Here was some horse indeed; before the season was out, he was to start at odds of 70–1 on! That was if an opponent could be found to take him on at all.

Next he was walked to Winchester races, this time for a prize of 100 guineas, when the opposi-

tion was Slouch, Chigger, Juba and Caliban; the prize was duly his, and for good measure he walked over for another 50 guineas race as well. Next stop was Salisbury, where it was the same story. With his reputation spreading like wildfire, he walked over for another 50 guineas and beat Sulphur and an unnamed six-year-old for just 30 guineas.

This wonder horse was surely unbeatable, the wags were saying. He travelled to Canterbury to pick up another 100 guineas unearned income, and on to Lewes, on the attractive Downs above the little county town of Sussex, folded into the narrow valley beneath them. There, Kingston took him on but saw only a distant view of his tail, and finally for that season Tardy was given similar treatment at Litchfield, both these wins earning 100 guineas each.

During the winter of 1769–70 Eclipse matured and filled out. He was still considered 'short in the forehand and high in the hips' and certainly did not have the best or most compact conformation in the world, but he did have the guts. He also 'possessed speed, stride, ability to carry weight, strength of wind and power of endurance never surpassed, if equalled', as Theo Taunton said in his book, *Famous Horses* (1895).

Naturally, all the racing world (except perhaps those looking for winning opportunities for inferior horses) were agog to see how Eclipse would reappear in 1770. As usual John Oakley was booked to ride, and as usual he wisely left Eclipse alone to run as he liked – and if that sometimes looked as if he was being run away with, well, he never forgot to pull up after the winning post was passed!

His reappearance race was the much more valuable 400 guineas race at Newmarket in April, his first visit to 'Headquarters'. Now the pundits could see what he was really made of. Ranged alongside him – or rather behind him, for that is all they saw of him – were Diana, Pensioner and Chigger. Eclipse really earned his oats at that meeting: as if the four-mile heats for that race weren't enough, he covered the distance several times more to win 150 guineas against Corsican – and then for good measure added two more walk-overs of 100 guineas each.

He was travelled further north this season, and on his way to York, which ranked second only behind Newmarket for quality of racing, he took

in a walk-over at Nottingham. Two 'capital run-ners', Bellario and Tortoise, took him on at York, but they were made to look like common work-horses as they struggled more than a distance behind him from two miles on. It was as always a case of the further Eclipse went, the more he liked it.

The nearest he ever got to an opponent worthy of the name was the north's Bucephalus, by Regulus, run at level weights at Newmarket (April). Scribes of the time recorded, 'Bucephalus ran like a good and true son of Regulus but he never afterwards regained his form, so severe and heartbreaking were the efforts he made on that occasion.' It is a story which has occasionally been repeated down through horseracing's history.

The York race proved to be Eclipse's last against opponents. His season – and career, for what was the point of continuing when none would race against him – ended with 100-guinea walk-overs at Lincoln and Guildford. With a sigh of relief from his opponents, he was retired, unbeaten, having won 2149 guineas and never felt the whip or a spur.

How many people, when quoting his eighteen successive victories, realize that half of them were walk-overs? Or conversely, that those which did have opposition were in effect several races because of the daunting system of running each race in several heats?

It can happen that a horse with a reputation scares away the opposition to such an extent that

OPPOSITE

Top *Eclipse first, the rest nowhere . . . seen here with his jockey John Oakley.*

Bottom *The influence of Eclipse as a stallion was great. He sired three of the first five Derby winners.*

in the end he is virtually beating only those running for the place money. It happened with Lottery, winner of the first Grand National in 1839, and with Arkle in the 1960s, both of whom had the framing of races changed because of them.

But the proof of the pudding is in the eating, and it was at stud that Eclipse was truly immortalized. Unlike some modern Thoroughbreds who are rushed off to stud the moment they win the Derby lest their record be tarnished by defeat later, Eclipse was truly the greatest horse of his time, as shown emphatically by his stud record, comparable with Herod, Matchem and Highflyer. He sired three of the first five Derby winners, that race being founded on his home track ten years after his retirement; he sired the winners of 862 races; and most of the greatest horses in the history of horseracing trace back to him.

At Clay Hill Stud, Epsom, his prize money having barely covered O'Kelly's purchase price, he commanded a fee of 50 guineas, which even in old age never dropped below 30, earning £25,000 for Colonel O'Kelly. By the time Theodore Cook's book *Eclipse and O'Kelly* was published in 1907, eighty-two of the 127 Derby winners were his direct descendants. O'Kelly was not, Cook claims, the ruffian of obscure origin he has been made out to be, having left Ireland as a young man to seek his fortune, but had learned 'a good Italian hand'.

Eclipse was twenty-five years old when, on 25 February 1789, he contracted colic. For two days he fought for his life, but in spite of the best care and treatment available, he died at 7 p.m. on 27 February. His skeleton was donated to the Natural History Museum and is currently on loan to the National Horseracing Museum at Newmarket. How many of the 27,000 annual visitors there, I wonder, have noticed that two of his vertebrae are fused?

A Good Place for a Picnic

Royal Ascot

It is Gold Cup day at Royal Ascot, 1988. Everywhere the sense of occasion and anticipation is high. Picnics are spread, champagne corks pop, hats are adjusted and the rails are lined awaiting the Royal Procession.

How Queen Anne, who suffered so much in her short life, would smile if she could see the pleasure her purchase of the heath for £558 19s 5d in 1711 to make a racecourse has brought to her subjects' descendants.

Queen Anne, who founded racing at Ascot.

At the time she had only three years to live and was in constant pain through ill-health. She had borne seventeen children, not one of whom survived to adulthood. Affairs of state and the war against France were conducted with the help of the Duke of Marlborough, an able statesman, while financial affairs were the responsibility of her Lord Treasurer, Godolphin – all this nearly twenty years before one Edward Coke imported an Arabian horse from Paris which was later acquired by the 2nd Earl of Godolphin. The Godolphin Arabian became one of the three famous progenitors of the Thoroughbred, along with the Byerley Turk and the Darley Arabian.

Queen Anne is said to have preferred hunting to racing, enthusiastically following her Royal Buckhounds through Windsor Forest in a chaise pulled by a fast horse. One can imagine some hairy and exhilarating moments! It seems strange, in view of her evident love of the chase, that in *The Lives of the Kings and Queens of England*, edited by Antonia Fraser, Queen Anne is said to have enjoyed playing cards, drinking tea and admiring gardens but 'loathed fresh air'. Whatever the truth, there is no disputing that when she arranged for a Queen's Plate to be contested in July 1711 on her newly acquired 'Ascott Heath', it was a sporting occasion with a picnic atmosphere enjoyed by her friends.

More than anywhere else, outside point-to-points, that tradition thrives today. And what picnics! A veritable feast is produced from some of the smartest cars in the country; top-hatted and tail-coated gentlemen more used to expensive West End business lunches can be seen tucking in from their car boots, accompanied by their ladies, many in high heels and even higher fashion.

The vast heath, dotted by clumps of stunted oaks, silver birch and bushes, has cars parked all over it at varying angles: some occupants just

Top *The Oatlands Sweepstakes, 1791, won by the Prince of Wales's Barnet. This was the fastest race at Ascot during the eighteenth century and attracted a crowd of over 40,000 people.*

Above *As this picture shows, fashion has always been a highlight of Royal Ascot. This was the scene in the Enclosure before the Ascot Gold Cup of 1895.*

spread a rug on the ground and use plastic mugs and plates; others produce the finest glassware, silver and crockery with lavish tables and chairs. All enjoy the atmosphere and food in their own way, whether they are having lobster, caviar, salmon, strawberries and champagne, or run-of-the-mill sandwiches and strawberries and champagne.

A painting by Henry Alken of Ascot in 1822 which carried the caption: 'Tom and Bob winning the long odds from a knowing one.'

Nor is this the only feasting, because for four days Royal Ascot offers a feast of racing too. There are those who believe the Epsom Derby meeting should be reduced to two days, or even one, because of the poor quality of the supporting programme. When one compares it with the card for Royal Ascot, where nearly every race has group status, it is easy to see why. Epsom happens to host the world's greatest, most prestigious horserace. Royal Ascot has just about everything else.

Plans to visit Royal Ascot have to be made well in advance, especially by those wishing to be accommodated in the Royal Enclosure. Here the rules are nearly as traditional as the racing, and although they are not as tight as they once were (until 1955 divorced men were segregated in a corner on their own, for instance), certain standards must still be adhered to.

The time is approaching two; eyes cast anxiously upwards note with relief that today the ever-fickle British weather looks set fair. Many of the picnics, or rather their remnants, are left spread across the grass or draped over car bonnets, for it is time for the Royal Procession. There are five carriages in all (there were seven in 1838, when Queen Victoria attended), headed by the one conveying the Queen, Prince Philip and Prince Charles, pulled by the Windsor greys, set off to perfection by the scarlet-liveried outriders, as they jog up the broad green sward towards the Golden Gates that take them into the Royal Enclosure.

There is a special cheer for the Duchess of York, who is expecting her first baby, and for the Princess of Wales, but the biggest cheer of all is reserved for the Queen Mother. The Royal Procession is a tradition that was started by George IV when he came to the throne in 1820, only seven years after one of the Enclosures Acts, under which Ascot Heath was assigned to the king subject that 'it should be kept and continued as a racecourse for the public use at all times as it has usually been'.

The royal party alight from their carriages at the Golden Gates and walk, shoulder to shoulder with the crowds, to the royal box in the grandstand built in 1961. The catering in the members' stand and for those with private boxes is superb, if expensive. Racecourses do not have the best reputation in the world in this respect, long queues for mediocre, overpriced, mass-produced food being all too often the norm, while to obtain a drink is to survive the argy-bargy of a cattle-market crush, only to pay through the nose for the privilege.

Perhaps racegoers should try complaining more often; in the 1840s at Ascot, the price of luncheon was actually reduced from half a sovereign to 7s. The 'ten bob' offer had been for 'the mummy of a rusty old rook' but a 'very fair cold collation'

could be had for 3s 6d! A change of caterer in the 1860s meant it became possible to get a 'pigeon pie that was not all beef' and a 'lobster salad in which there was some lobster'!

Back to today, and the place is bursting at the seams; for a good many of the 69,000 visitors, the social aspect is all; ladies who try to outshine the rest with their fashion, men who try to outdrink others in the bars. By contrast, for the racing

buff, there is four days of the best horseflesh on view; and for others it is a combination of enjoying dressing up and meeting friends and of admiring the horses.

In truth, the Royal Enclosure, grandstand and

The elegant fashions of the 1980s, as worn in the Royal Enclosure.

Be prepared for crowds – and not many spare square inches – when visiting Royal Ascot today.

paddock areas are a teeming throng and a bit like a rugger scrum, and even though there is room to move in the Silver Ring, it is not easy to see. But across the course lies 'the best value in racing', the heath enclosure, which costs just £1 to get in; here there is room to move and plenty of opportunity to see. And plenty of folk have put on their best dresses and hats too; it is 'their' day, just as much as it is for the 'toffs' on the other side.

There are the gypsies selling 'lucky' heather, the ticket touts, the ubiquitous hot-dog and ice-cream vans, and a man covered from head to foot in badges topped by a huge Red Indian headdress; there is a long line of bookmakers, a tea room with further tables and chairs outside, enough loos – and there is room.

More picnics spread here like Druids' circles on the grass; the canny have brought folding chairs up with them from the car park, and they settle down for the afternoon in the sunshine. Some of the men strip to their shorts, but by and large there is a sense of occasion on the heath too. They get a good view of the Royal Procession and of the 'nobs' on the 'other side'; they can watch the horses leave the paddock and canter to the start; and they can get a very fair view of the racing, right on the finishing line.

It is Thursday, traditionally ladies' day, and Handsome Sailor is favourite for the first, the group 3 Cork and Orrery Stakes over six furlongs.

Picnics are very much part and parcel of the Royal Ascot scene.

But the chestnut is sweating profusely and can finish only sixth behind the 11–2 chance Posada, owned by Mrs Bruce Bossom in partnership with Jockey Club member and successful point-to-point rider Tim Holland-Martin, who also bred him at his Overbury Stud in the Cotswolds.

But it is the favourite's turn in the five furlongs group 3 Norfolk Stakes as the superbly named Superpower adds a sixth consecutive victory to his name with the ease that such a record suggests.

The day's highlight is the 2½-mile Gold Cup – or it should be. Sadly, this year it turns into one of the most disputed races in the history of the Turf, starting a press debate to match any other ever known. The Gold Cup was founded in 1807 for 100 guineas with a sweepstake of 10 guineas. When Tsar Nicholas I of Russia visited Ascot in 1845, he presented a £500 plate, known as the Emperor's Plate, but when the Crimean War broke out nine years later, it seemed prudent to revert to the Gold Cup.

Sagaro won the race a record three times, and twelve have won it twice, including those great stayers Le Moss (1979–80) and Ardross in 1981 and 1982, when he gave Lester Piggott his eleventh success in the race, his first having been on Zarathustra in 1957. Triple Crown winners such as West Australian, who set the then record time in 1854, Gladiateur, who won by forty lengths in 1866, and then in 1895 possibly the greatest racehorse of all time, beaten only once, Isinglass, whose stake earnings record stood until 1952, all added their names to the role of honour. Neither should mention of St Simon in 1884, Persimmon in 1897 and Bayardo in 1910 be omitted.

It was only in 1987 that geldings were admitted, otherwise Brown Jack's name would surely be added to the scroll, but instead he made the longest flat race of all his own, the 2¾-mile Queen Alexandra Stakes, run on the Friday of Royal Ascot, which he won a remarkable six years in succession from 1929 to 1934.

Ironically, the horse at the centre of the 1988 Gold Cup dispute was none other than a gelding, Royal Gait. There were thirteen runners for the race, including one each from France, Norway and Ireland; there were several Arab owners and

*Royal Gait,
controversially
disqualified from the
Ascot Gold Cup of 1988.*

the owner of the French-trained Royal Gait was a Spaniard, Manuel Periear Arias; the horse was ridden by the American Cash Asmussen – all adding to the truly international flavour of Britain's most prestigious race outside the classics.

In the event, it was Royal Gait who broke the course record by three seconds (previously set by Gildoran in 1984) in his convincing five lengths' win, after El Conquistador had set such a blistering pace that even this out-and-out stayer could not sustain it. He tired and was headed three furlongs out when, as Royal Gait tried to come past him two furlongs from home, contact was made between the two and El Conquistador's jockey, Tony Clark, was unseated.

The stewards contended that Royal Gait did not have room to come through between the fatigued early leader and that horse's stable companion,

OPPOSITE
The Royal Procession is a tradition which began with George IV when he came to the throne in 1820. Princess Margaret and the Duchess of York enjoy the welcoming applause of the huge crowds in 1988 (top) and the Queen, accompanied by the Duke of Edinburgh and Sheikh Abdullah, acknowledges the warm reception (bottom).

Sadeem, the favourite, next to him, and that Royal Gait's jockey should not have tried to.

The art of jockeyship is all about finding ways to get out without impeding other horses. To read some of the press reports and their unqualified criticism of the stewards, one would not have thought so. It had the ring of the 1913 Derby about it, when that race was marred not only by the fatal action of suffragette Emily Davison, who threw herself in the path of King George V's Anmer at Tattenham Corner, but also by the disqualification of Craganour.

On that occasion there was undoubtedly a good deal of bumping and boring. A strike from the whip made Craganour veer towards Aboyeur, who in turn tried to savage Craganour; Aboyeur swung towards the rails, hampering another runner, then veered out again, hanging on to Craganour; the scrap continued all the way to the post, with Craganour getting up by a head. Instead of there being a Stewards' Inquiry, as happens today, the stewards lodged an objection, making them both prosecutors and arbiters. Few, if any, thought Craganour would lose the race; indeed, the bookies, who usually have the right answer in these things, offered up to 5–1 on Aboyeur getting it. But in a hasty fifteen minutes

the result came: Aboyeur was awarded the race and Craganour placed last. Newspaper reports left readers convinced that the stewards, one of whom had a long-standing bitterness against Craganour's connections, had been blind with prejudice, bias and favouritism.

Certainly the 1988 affair left a sad and sour taste to what should have been a fine victory. Royal Gait was disqualified and placed last and Cash Asmussen was disqualified for seven days, penalties that were upheld by a much-publicized subsequent appeal to the Jockey Club Stewards in Portman Square. The race went to Sadeem, not only favourite but also stable companion to the faller, trained by Guy Harwood in Sussex.

Cash Asmussen immediately followed up this débâcle by winning the next race, the group 2 Ribblesdale Stakes, on Paul Kelleway's Miss Boniface. The only disappointment for the crowds here was that a royal victory had looked in prospect as the Queen's Highbrow hit the front two furlongs out but had no answer for the eventual winner.

The betting shock of the day came in the listed Chesham Stakes, won by 50–1 outsider Jacamar, but there was even more drama to come in the last race. Greville Starkey, awarded the Gold Cup on Sadeem, had the concluding King George V Stakes handicap 'sewn up', only for his mount, Ile de Chypre, to duck suddenly sideways just 100 yards from home, ignominiously dumping his rider on the turf.

It had been a day to remember, a day of triumph and disaster, as slowly the bars' flow of champagne dried up and the crowds queued to get

Ile de Chypre swerves and unseats jockey Greville Starkey within sight of the winning post in the King George V Stakes handicap.

out (exit made easier by the superb organization), until only the litter was left, to be doggedly cleared up in time for the next day's card, the whole process to be repeated the next evening . . .

The day's end. All that remains is for the litter to be cleared.

Mantraps at Manton

The famous training establishment

If Alec Taylor and his son, who between them trained twenty-eight classic winners from Manton, near Marlborough, Wiltshire, after creating it from scratch in the 1890s, were to return today, they would on first glance see little changed. Their house is still an integral part of the Victorian yard, the courtyard is still immaculately kept, the caged boxes are unaltered and the central gas lamp is just as Alec senior left it, off centre so that he could see anyone arriving into the square from his windows.

But transport him just 100 yards to one side and his eyes would pop out of his head at the 'space age' vision in front of him. For Manton today is a true mixture of ancient and modern. Subject to a facelift in the 1980s, its new Astor yard and offices complex is quite unlike any other in Britain, built along scientific lines with no detail spared.

Mirrored glass prevents any prying eyes from peering into the new yard complex, dominated by an ultra-modern house and offices. The yard itself is a mixture of forty English-style boxes and twenty in an American-style barn, as well as huge hay and fodder stores. Trace heating runs through all the boxes and outside each is a kit cupboard which also includes a water meter. There are two isolation yards with four boxes in each. All under cover are the drying-room, head lad's office, racing-tack room, solarium, scales, trotting-up area, rooms for X-rays, scopes, lasers, ultra-sound and magnetopulse treatments, a darkroom for processing, a pharmacy, a veterinary examining area and a wash-down room, some of which have now been converted to extra stables. A digital clock/thermometer contrasts with the traditional clock-tower that tops the entrance to the old yard.

To the rear of the new buildings is an attractive lake with two separate covered lungeing yards on each side of it, and close by is a mechanical horse exerciser.

Manton is owned by Robert Sangster, who, in the early 1980s, decided he would have to centralize his racing empire. In his heyday as an owner in the 1970s, before the Arabs arrived and stamped their mark so indelibly on British racing, Robert Sangster had at one time had twenty-three different trainers. This was because when he bought a horse, rather than take it away from its current trainer to that man's inevitable disappointment, he would leave it *in situ*. What's more, he often then extended the relationship by buying yearlings for the trainer in future years.

His principal English trainers remained Barry Hills, Michael Stoute, Bill Watts, Charlie Nelson and Mick Easterby. Eventually, from a management point of view, the whole thing became too unwieldy, so Sangster decided to acquire his own yard and install a private trainer: hence Manton and the mastermind behind its transformation, Michael Dickinson.

The existing trainers were not simply sacked: they were told that there would be no more yearlings the following year, effectively giving each trainer two years' notice, and a number were still to be retained with Barry Hills.

Michael Dickinson, still a young man, had reached the top of the National Hunt training tree, having been a successful jockey before that. The trainer of the first five home in Bregawn's Cheltenham Gold Cup of 1983, a feat most unlikely to be attempted again, let alone bettered, he had headed the trainers' list three times and achieved the record of training twelve winners in one day, on Boxing Day, 1982, at several different meetings. He accepted Robert Sangster's offer to come to Manton and, given a more or less free hand, set about making it the most scientifically advanced training establishment, at least in Britain.

It was not to prove a long association and during his second season of training, Michael

The new Astor yard and offices complex, built in the 1980s along scientific lines.

Robert Sangster (left) who bought Manton in the early 1980s, seen here with John Hills.

turned his skills towards America, setting up in Pennsylvania. So it was quite out of the blue that fifty-year-old Barry Hills was offered the replacement job at the end of 1986. Already a long-standing friend, as well as trainer, for Robert Sangster, he packed up shop in Lambourn, during that winter took his 100 horses to join Sangster's sixty at Manton, set about getting to know them and the set-up in double quick time – and ended up with his best ever season, which included training the winner of the Irish Derby, Sir Harry Lewis.

There was more to it than that, for although Robert Sangster had loyally promised him the same *number* of horses at Lambourn in 1986, it was naturally to his new private trainer Michael Dickinson that he sent what was considered the cream, and that included members of several equine families Barry had known and nurtured for years. Whereas the public gets to know longer-lasting National Hunt horses better, it is in the *breeding* that so much of the fascination lies for those involved in the flat. With shorter racecourse lives and quicker breeding cycles, it is easy to see sons, grandsons and even great-grandsons or daughters emulating their forebears. So Barry was

Barry Hills, who trains at Manton, principally for Robert Sangster.

reunited with many of 'his' families, and they prospered.

Lying as it does to the west of Marlborough, away from any of the large training environs, Manton is very much a self-contained entity, complete with its own 'village' and all that goes to make up a community. There are eighty-four members of staff, many of whom are housed with their families on the estate, where there is also a postbox and phone box.

Cricket is played on the large green outside the houses of Taylor's Court (the new ones have three bedrooms and two bathrooms), there is a keenly contested tennis tournament, fishing takes place on the lake and children's sports are organized. There is a 'pub' in the Manton House yard and a games room which has been there since the property was bought by developer Mr John Bloomfield for his private parties, renting the yard to George Peter-Hoblyn. It is said that three Derby winners were stabled overnight at the Green Dragon Inn in nearby Marlborough prior to boarding trains to take them to Epsom.

Much remains the same as in the days of old, when Alec Taylor junior was twelve times champion trainer, although the old chapel is now derelict. When it was in use, a flock of sheep used to be herded into the basement on a Saturday night to warm it up in time for Sunday services. Bayardo, who won the 1909 St Leger, is buried nearby, and his rather worn hide adorns the seat of the jockeys' scales.

Manton House yard, never used by Michael Dickinson, is fully operational again and with what was built as a yearling barn, known as the Barton yard, now making up a third training

The old yard at Manton, home to generations of classic winners.

Barry Hills (arm raised) overseeing his string on the Clatford gallops.

yard, there is plenty of friendly rivalry between them, complete with a 'scoreboard'. Each has its own assistant trainer and Barry gives them every chance with as little interference in the day-to-day running as possible. Interestingly, the three yards boast roughly the same number of winners each, in spite of their huge differences in style, a tremendous compliment to Barry Hills. Of course, they have their gallops in common – and what gallops! Manton is surely one of the most beautiful of English settings, and to live and work there is a delight, especially in the summer.

In the Taylors' heyday, the then 5000-acres estate (it is about half that now) boasted that it could gallop horses on replicas of every single racecourse in Britain! There would be thirty to forty apprentices from Manchester indentured. Joe Lawson, who had been assistant there, added to the tally of Manton-trained classic winners, and between the wars the yard was bought by the auctioneering firm Tattersall's. They sold it after the war to George Todd, who turned out one classic winner, Psidium, in the Irish Derby, before it passed on to Mr Bloomfield and from him to the last incumbent, Robert Baker, who did not have much luck, with just a handful of horses.

Now Barry Hills rides his hunter as his trainer's hack, and from his vantage point he can watch whatever piece of work has been chosen for that day. In all, there are some 500 acres of gallops, although once they went all the way to Ogbourne, and a further 500 acres of nature conservancy; the remainder is all farmed in hand, with about 1000 ewes being stocked.

No horse will ever get bored at Manton, for he never knows which way he will be turning from his box, and the sheer variety is enormous; even the early season 'road work' can be achieved entirely off tarmac and on the tracks and bridle-ways crisscrossing the estate. A peat moss gallop was made by Michael Dickinson and two all-weathers; the six-furlong moss gallop is almost *too* good, so much does it resemble a racecourse, complete with white rails. One all-weather is a flat six-furlong circle and the other winds its way around the farmland on one side of the long entrance drive, a U-shaped nine furlongs, three on the flat, then a good uphill pull for another three before levelling out for the final three.

The actual gallops total eighteen miles and every inch of them can be watered; all have been renovated and one thing Michael Dickinson did was to 'bank' a bend, making it resemble an American track (English horses increasingly visit that country these days). This is on the Clatford gallop, enabling horses to gallop flat out round the bend, an exhilarating experience for the jockey on top! A replica of Belmont, USA, it is also a useful training for Tattenham Corner, and both Robert Sangster and Michael Dickinson went to great lengths to perfect its construction.

Michael also had some 30,000 trees and shrubs planted around the place, although they do not provide the same amount of cover as there used to

be beside the Valley gallop, where the important trials were held in the old days. Then, there used to be mantraps laid in the woods alongside to try and deter the touts! From here there is the Derby gallop in the distance, a straight seven furlongs which rises 150 feet and is named after two Derby winners who did their last piece of work there in Alec Taylor junior's time.

In the Stoney valley are Sarsen stones, to which people still come to take rubbings. The Clatford gallop is the main one; apart from the banked bend, it has a five-furlong straight uphill, off which there are six spurs, numbers five and six being steep, used for steady cantering, and numbers one, two and three being used for most of the galloping. On the top, set back from the rest, is Warren Wood, where riding is cool in summer and warm in winter, another enviable change of scene for the horses.

It is little wonder that so many of the staff stayed on when Barry Hills came. The tingling atmosphere of the whole place is immediately apparent, with its unique blend of history, pride and tradition, mixed with the sense of being part of a great future.

Manton, probably the best equipped training establishment in Britain, boasts eleven separate gallops, including two all-weather ones.

Lucky To Be Alive

A trainer gets started

If Manton boasts probably the most technologically advanced training establishment in Britain, and Newmarket houses such show places as Henry Cecil's Warren Place and Lord Derby's Stanley House (but sadly no longer the most historic of all, Palace House Stables, now empty and decaying behind the High Street), there is always room for the small-timer too, and who is to say his part is not just as important?

Certainly the atmosphere and 'rusticness' of Dr Jon Scargill's Albert House Stables was immediately apparent. Although they are yards from the clock-tower at the end of the High Street and behind a garage, with most of the approach taken up by secondhand cars for sale, once in the yard it is secluded and 'countrified', with birds singing their hearts out, something I did not notice at the plush Hamilton Road set-ups.

Albert House is in fact one of the oldest yards in Newmarket. The stable walls are lined with two-inch metal strips, like those found in Beckhampton, to stop the horses eating the wood or kicking the walls down, and they have cage doors and brick tile floors. The mellow outside brick walls are set off by stable doors painted a warm, rich red, and if some of them needed a lick more, or a spot of rehanging, that would come when Jon Scargill achieved the success of which he was certain.

Far from the orthodox racing man, not the son of a trainer and certainly never an apprentice, he did not learn to ride until his mid-twenties. Jon Scargill is a doctor in biochemistry – and is lucky to be alive at all. He grew up in Gravesend, an industrialized part of Kent that could hardly be further removed from racing, with parents who were teachers and had no interest in the sport. But like so many others before him, Jon's imagination was caught, and from the age of four or five, as soon as he could read, he pored over the form on the racing pages. At school, the local grammar, he

methodically used to keep a diary of the bets he would have made and the profits or losses they would have brought him. 'It was a passion rather than a hobby, and always ran parallel with my school work as a separate thing.'

Although he loved it (the first racecourse he visited was Newton Abbott when on holiday in the West Country), he never imagined racing would become his life: instead, he progressed to the University of London to read biochemistry and it was assumed he would become a lecturer. Only when he went on from there for a PhD at Cambridge and moved into a house at Newmarket did a new plan begin to take shape: he determined to become a trainer. But how to gain an entrance into the closed world to which he was strictly an outsider?

His young wife, Sue, thought she had seen somewhere that Bruce Hobbs, youngest ever winner of the Grand National and later a top Newmarket trainer, had given a young trainer a start, and she wrote to him. 'With your qualifications, why don't you apply to the Equine Research Station?' came the predictable reply. But Jon wanted the real thing; biochemistry called for frustratingly slow results and too much minute detail for his temperament; he persuaded Bruce Hobbs to let him work at evening stables for nothing, to gain some experience. Thus he got his foot on the first rung of the ladder, leaving at 5 a.m. each morning to cycle the fifteen miles to college in Cambridge in order to be back in time to 'do his two'.

He was about eighteen months into his PhD when his whole life nearly collapsed about him: working on a thesis on mosquito toxins, he accidentally injected himself. As his arm swelled and the poison was reaching ever more dangerously close to his heart, he was rushed to hospital, but of course, he was the only person in the country

Albert House Stables, where Jon Scargill began training with just nine horses.

who had any knowledge of his work and baffled doctors were in a quandary. Luckily, Jon did not lose consciousness and was able to pinpoint the most likely antibiotics.

In the end, he was 'pumped full of everything' and recovered, but it was a close shave. Happily, the effective insecticide which was the result of his research into why a bacterially produced protein remained inert until it was activated inside the gut of a mosquito, is now used all over Africa.

But still it was racing that drew him away from the academic life. 'With horses you are always learning, they keep telling me something, they are pure science.' So Sue and he hatched their plan. 'There must be some way to get into racing,' they thought.

When he was given his PhD, with his initial experience behind him, he joined Sir Mark Prescott as a pupil assistant trainer. A 'hard, stern man', he knocked the rough edges off his undeterred pupil. After about a year, he moved on, determined to catch up on lost time and to keep learning. This time, he answered an advertisement from Mouse Morris in Ireland, who was looking for an assistant trainer. Naturally, the well-known jump trainer asked for a reference. Fearing his lack of riding ability would be found out, Jon said, 'Obviously I would only send you a good reference, why don't you let me come over

for two weeks' trial instead?'

So, leaving Sue earning their bread in England, he embarked on his visit to Ireland, having hurriedly crammed in a couple of lessons at the local riding school – hardly the same thing as sitting on a Thoroughbred, as he soon discovered. 'The lads quickly sussed out that I couldn't really ride, and loved putting me on something that would give them a good laugh as I was being run away with!' He adds, 'It was a marvellous experience. The Irish just love horses and Mouse asked me to stay, but Newmarket is the centre of racing and I felt I had to be there.'

He returned to Headquarters as assistant to Robert Williams, who then had twenty-eight horses but now has over seventy; Jon learned more again, including office work, dealing with owners at the races and so on in his eighteen months. By then he was ready for more; he had seen the training of sellers and handicappers, and Robert Williams had an exceptionally high win strike rate with his two-year-olds. Now he wanted to observe the preparation of potential classic horses, and he joined Luca Cumani. 'The classic prospects are treated differently from day one,' he says, 'and

ideally I would have stayed there two years to see their programme right through.'

But with few yards available to rent in New-market, when the chance of Albert House came up it was too good an opportunity to miss. At one time it had been an overflow yard for Bruce Hobbs, then Tim Thomson Jones, and its most recent incumbent had been John Fitzgerald, the only lord training in Newmarket. So Jon and Sue, herself a teacher but then working at Tattersall's, and their baby son Peter moved in; joining them as head lad was Kevin Merry, who, at Cumani's, had looked after Kahyasi. It meant, less than a year later, that Kevin missed out on the best pay day of his life when that smashing colt won the Derby, for 2 per cent of the £228,700 winnings would have come his way. 'But he made the right choice,' says Jon. 'He's a super bloke who will go far.'

The first thing Jon discovered on setting up on his own was that of a dozen 'cast-iron' owners who had promised him horses, only two actually sent them. But he received his mixed licence in February and had his first runner in March 1988 in a hurdle at Worcester. His first runner on the flat, Magic Milly, was beaten by a head at Newcastle and by June he had had his first winner, the well-named Four Legged Friend; from his first twelve runners, six were placed; two more winners over one weekend quickly followed and his yard was full, with twenty-six horses. By the end of that first season in 1988 he had trained nine winners.

For his owners, the emphasis is on enjoyment and involvement; with his scientific approach, Jon likes to run horses only when he feels they have a realistic chance. As he says:

Racing is no longer gentlemen's leisure, but leisure is a business. There is no 'inner sanctum' mystery here; my owners are mostly successful small businessmen – sometimes they run horses to entertain clients or advertise their business, sometimes three of four friends club together for a horse or two.

Any owner supporting a first season trainer is taking a risk, but I'm not a gambling man: the odds are with me ...

I've mortgaged my house and wife and dog to do it, what's more!

Within a year, Jon Scargill (right), *already a success, had expanded to a new purpose-built yard in Hamilton Road* (below right), *with 48 boxes built and planning permission for a total of 96.*

The 'Monkey on a Stick'

Tod Sloan, 1874-1933

Like poor Fred Archer's, Tod Sloan's career was destined to be all too short, but for a different reason. The importer to England of the 'monkey on a stick' style of race riding, he could handle the ridicule with which he was first greeted, but he could not cope with what he saw as the 'sour grapes' attitude of the autocratic Jockey Club. In banning him for betting, he was almost certainly being made a scapegoat, and not only was his career ruined but in many respects so was his life.

Born in Indiana in 1874 of humble stock and brought up by adoptive parents who did not so much as drive a donkey, let alone ride a horse, Tod Sloan, as he became known, was a most unlikely person to become a famous jockey on both sides of the Atlantic before the turn of the century. From playing truant at school, he was 'to show the world how weight could be properly distributed on a horse'. He was to amass nearly half a million pounds and to meet every celebrity in the world.

The company he mixed with as a boy was of a different sort; he always remembered Buffalo Bill (Colonel Cody of *Annie Get Your Gun* fame) being kind to him and bouncing him on his knee, and another acquaintance he remembered was Frank James, brother of Jesse, both bandits, and the fascination with guns he then acquired remained with him always.

His first experience of horses was enough to put anyone off for life, and it nearly did in his case. Wanting to get to a friend's funeral some distance away, he 'borrowed' a horse, which was quite likely unbroken, put his feet through the leathers because the irons were too long and proceeded to be 'carted' at an ever increasing pace, so that, in his words, it was lucky there did not end up being two funerals. By a strange coincidence, in his effort to stay on the horse, he flung his arms round its neck, crouching forward to do so – the

Tod Sloan at the turn of the century.

very 'style' that was to make him so famous in later years.

Tod, in fact, did not take the credit for inventing the new crouch style; that accolade went to Harry Griffin, for ever, in Tod's mind, one of the best and most underrated of jockeys. Tod saw

Contrasting styles. Tom Loates (left) with the old-fashioned English style and American Tod Sloan, the 'monkey on a stick'.

him riding short and leaning over his horses, and, as he says in his autobiography, 'He was the best jockey of the day, and so I put two and two together.'

At the time, Tod was emphatically failing in his bid to become a jockey; he was so hopeless that 'if a trainer didn't want a horse to win, there was no need to give instructions to "pull" it, he only had to put up Tod Sloan'! In fact by 1894 he was thinking of quitting and taking up the stage (he was later to marry an actress), until the day when he rode a horse at Bay District track. It tried to bolt with him on the way to the start, and in trying to get it back to him, Tod got up out of the saddle and on to the horse's neck; he laughed at himself, yet noticed that the horse's stride seemed to be freer, and he found it easier for him too.

It was some time before he had the courage of his convictions and for a while he simply kept practising at home. 'At last, though, I really did spring it on them. Everybody laughed, they thought I'd turned into a comedian, but I was too cocksure to be discouraged.'

The result was that, at last, he began to win races. He displayed a born understanding of horses and their temperaments and mastered the knack of 'kidding' a reluctant horse. He learned that horses run best when 'pocketed', so that the air does not rush at them, and that even the most tired horse will find that little bit extra if he can have a 'guide' on each side of him, either rails and horse or two horses, at the end of a race.

People began to sit up and take notice of him. In 1896, Tom Loates, a crack English jockey, visited America and Tod took him under his wing, tipping him winners that he was riding. They were generally having a good time together. So he felt somewhat aggrieved when he found his friend quoting various other American jockeys, but not him as the best, in a newspaper interview. It made him determined to get to England and ride against its aces to see who really was the best. His chance came the next season.

It was a lonely, homesick young man who descended on Newmarket with no friends and, to begin with, no rides. His first two were 'no-hopers' and his 'monkey' style was laughed out of court; sportswriters let their pens loose on his supposed limitations.

It was the year tape starts were used for the first time experimentally at Newmarket, but Tod had had a couple of years' experience back home and he lost no time in gaining his revenge. 'When the barrier flew up and the others were getting ready, I was nearly a quarter finished!' he recalled.

He had come to England to ride St Cloud for Lord William Beresford, a man who had implicit faith in the American, but Tod was amazed at the severity of the training compared with that in his home country. His pre-Cesarewitch wind-up 'canter' on the Limekilns at Newmarket (where important work is still carried on today, usually on a Saturday) 'was more like a four-mile gallop', recorded Tod, who was then flabbergasted to find he was next supposed to gallop the horse.

For all the discomfort he felt in a strange land, Tod was impressed with the way jockeys were treated: they were given luncheon vouchers and the officials all seemed pleasant. As his reputation grew, so did his stature; his style was proving a winning one and inevitably, for all the initial ridicule, it was soon being imitated.

He met not only the top lords and gentlemen of the land but also the future King of England, Edward, Prince of Wales. His empathy with horses, especially bad-tempered or sulky ones, also won him friends, and he was an early exponent of the art of riding a waiting race from in front. He would not ride in spurs and seldom used a whip.

At one time it was suggested that his style was 'unfair' and that he should carry a penalty! He pointed out that he was not so much riding short (others after him rode much, much shorter) as crouching forward, altering the whole balance and enabling a horse to use its speed and action to better effect. 'Hands and brain have more to do with successful race riding than anything else,' he surmised. After four wins and a second in one day at Manchester, his fans tried to mob him as he left the course, eager to pat his back or shake his hand. It took a dozen policemen to escort him safely into a waiting cab. In that one month he had ridden twenty-one winners from just forty-eight mounts.

It looked as if the world was at his feet, but there were dark clouds on the horizon. He was not the only American doing well; several trainers were coming over and they were scooping up a lot of races. The English, believing themselves invincible, were sure that there must be foul play afoot;

the word 'dope' was bandied about increasingly. There was disquiet among the English and an uncomfortable atmosphere. Certain inquiries would be made, they let it be known – and one of them was into the activities of Tod Sloan.

Writing in his autobiography, Tod stressed that he received only his riding fees as earnings; he never charged fees for gallops or travelling expenses but, like many others, he used to bet a little. When he was hauled before the Stewards in 1900, he readily admitted that he backed horses he was riding himself, thinking that, as in America, this was allowed. He was retiring anyway for that season and returning home. It was well known, he said, that many British jockeys bet 'and not all in half sovereigns'. He believed the reprimand he received was the end of the matter, as long as he did not digress again.

Not a bit of it. Not only was his licence not renewed in 1901 but it was never renewed again. Year after year, Tod reapplied. Every time his licence was refused. Many words condemning his behaviour were published then, and have been since.

Perhaps not surprisingly, it played on his mind. Tod began a business with new-fangled automobiles which failed; he unwisely took an action against the equivalent of the French Jockey Club and, although he won, it cost him dear, in terms of money and prospects in Britain; in 1909, when helping a friend in Belgium, he was promised a training licence in that country only to have it torn up in front of his eyes when he was suspected of race rigging.

The anti-American feeling reached its peak in 1913, when Britain introduced the Jersey Act, effectively reducing most American horses to half-bred status and rendering them ineligible for British racing overnight. It was a case of 'If you can't beat 'em, rule 'em out', and amazingly it was not repealed until 1949.

In 1915 the tenacious Tod Sloan applied yet again for his licence to ride. After three months, he had still had no reply. By this time he was working with ambulances in the First World War. He had ridden in England for only four seasons, and been cast aside for fifteen. 'A jockey's smiles are to be shared with the next fellow,' he said, 'but his tears are for himself.'

Tod Sloan died in 1933 in obscurity. But his name, and his style, live on.

The First Gentleman of Bookmaking

Archie Scott, 1904-65

Betting and racing go hand in hand; the Romans are said to have gambled wildly on their chariot racing, and the whole essence of racing is not just to see whose horse is best but to wager on the outcome. The first known bookmaker in England was one Mr Ogden from Lancashire, who set up at Newmarket in about 1795. Certainly, by 1856 a loose confederation of bookmakers had about 400 members. To begin with, when most races were matches, betting was largely between owners, originally in their own drawing-rooms, then increasingly in Tattersall's Subscription Rooms, or at a designated spot on a racecourse known as the betting-post.

In those early days, when bookmakers were known as 'blacklegs', they were almost to a man dishonest scoundrels. It is an image which has taken fully two and a half centuries to dispel, and the profession has certainly seen some chequered times. It became so disreputable in the early part of the nineteenth century that this period can truly be called the Dark Ages of the sport. The initial glamour and loftiness of racing's royal and noble beginnings had worn off; crowds were swelled by 'roughs' and drunkenness, debauchery and violence were rife; no woman could safely alight from her carriage and no gentleman could be certain his pocket would not be picked. Horses were doped or 'pulled', jockeys were bribed and any policing was hopelessly inadequate. Betting, particularly in pubs during Victorian times, became a national vice.

One outcome was that in the mid-nineteenth century off-course betting among the working classes was banned (while credit remained available for the upper classes), sending their business underground, not to be relegalized until 1961. This ban, along with other measures masterminded by Admiral Rous, contributed to the general clean-up of racing. Admiral Rous, the

Archie Scott, first gentleman of bookmaking.

third of racing's original 'dictators', was wholly averse to any shady betting. A Steward of the Jockey Club for over forty years, he became a sort of self-appointed perpetual president whose word was law, believing himself to be infallible – the sort of attitude that ultimately did not do the Jockey Club's name much good.

Racing's Golden Age was from about 1875 until

OPPOSITE

Top *Betting-posts were a common feature of race meetings in the early days.*

Bottom *Betting on Derby Day at Epsom one hundred years ago.*

the outbreak of the First World War, the war that was to change a whole way of life, any last remaining vestiges being wiped out by the Second World War. There was a post-war spree for a few years, but then an austere decade set in.

By the start of the decade that was to be dubbed the 'Swinging Sixties', racing desperately needed more money. Its foreign counterparts were forging ahead and the reason was obvious: they had a Tote monopoly, and because of it, much of the millions of pounds' betting turnover could be ploughed back into the sport – whereas in Britain it lined the bookmakers' pockets. Besides Britain, only Australia, Belgium, India and South Africa allow bookmakers at all. France made all bookmaking illegal way back in 1891. In some quarters of Britain, a Tote monopoly was considered the nearest thing to a racing certainty. Yet in spite – or because – of its anachronisms, Britain is a much-loved place throughout the world, with its great strength of character and depth of tradition, so no matter what the *logic* of a Tote monopoly, would not that 'little bit of something' be lost if bookmakers were banned? Racing would be richer in wealth but much poorer in colour.

One man in the profession above all others can be said to have saved the bookies: he was old Etonian Archie Scott, on Christian-name terms with Members and Stewards of the Jockey Club,

articulate, with a gentle and persuasive approach in putting the bookmakers' case across.

Standing 6 feet 6 inches high, Archie Scott, to those who knew him, was a pillar of society and as honest as the day, held in high regard and great esteem by people in all circles of racing. Without Archie, there is little doubt that Britain would have introduced a Tote monopoly. The profession has to thank the fates that led one star-struck Eton schoolboy into their ranks. Born in Scotland in 1904, the third of six sons of J. H. Scott, a family member of Scott's Shipbuilding on the Clyde, the tall, shy Archie could be expected to follow a pre-ordained path: Eton, Cambridge, Lloyd's, a good marriage.

All these things, in fact, he achieved, but he was only ten years old when his godmother, the Countess of Portarlington, took him to Sandown Park and he was bitten by the racing bug – and, as with others before and since, it was ultimately to hold sway.

It was when he was at Eton that Archie laid his first book – and very nearly came unstuck. It was 1920, Archie was sixteen, and the Derby was won by Spion Kop at 100–6. He just managed to pay out his chums, but it was a close-run thing. It did not deter him, though, and when he went up to Cambridge to read modern languages he found the lure of nearby Newmarket too tempting, and

Spion Kop, on whom sixteen-year-old Eton schoolboy Archie Scott laid his first book in 1920 when it won the Derby.

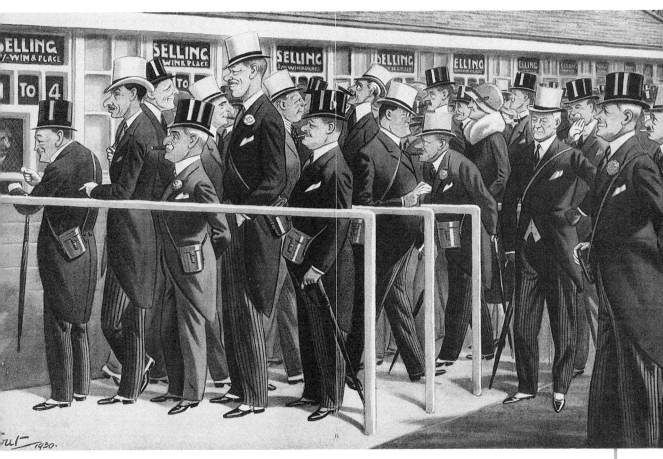

In 1930 the Tote operated at Epsom for the first time – thirty years later bookmakers were in danger of being ousted by it altogether.

soon he was paying someone else to attend college lectures for him. After Cambridge, he duly went into the City, but it was not the life for him. 'I almost went mad,' he said. 'It wasn't my idea of congenial work.'

He endured it for five years, then, to the shock and consternation of his bewildered mother, he went 'on the rails' as a clerk to bookmaker and former amateur billiards champion Sidney Fry in 1928. He said, 'My mother was a Victorian lady and it shook her to the roots. In certain houses, where I had been a guest, I was no longer welcome.'

Throughout his life, racecourses such as Ascot, Epsom and Goodwood would not allow him to become a member. His breeding was impeccable, but his profession, evidently, was not. In fact, he remained shy and reserved all his life, and found it hard when forced into the public glare during his negotiations with the Home Office and the Jockey Club prior to the Betting and Gaming Act of 1961.

Although some former 'friends' looked askance when he took up his new life, most did not and he continued to enjoy racing house-parties between the wars. He was part of racing's jet set, enjoying the time of their lives. In 1937 he married the Hon. Ruth Mary, daughter of the late 9th Viscount Downe, sister of the 10th Viscount Downe, Baron Dawnay. Archie loved racing with a passion, it was like a vocation to him, but he wouldn't let any of his four sons go into the business because they did not feel the same calling. The Dowager Lady Grimthorpe recalled those times in a letter to the *Sporting Life* in February 1988. Archie Scott

... had the highest standards and he lived up to them in every way. He and his partner and friend Peter Shepherd-Cross had one of the

most respected firms of bookmakers on the English Turf.

Archie and his wife Ruth, great personal friends of my husband, the late Lord Grimthorpe, and myself, stayed with us year after year for the May meeting at York. Archie would arrive, driving his beloved old Bentley, but Ruth came by train.

We had other friends to stay, played bridge or perhaps poker, and enjoyed ourselves. Next day, on the racecourse, there was Archie, standing up on the rails. I would go up to him to have a bet. Archie would take off his hat and say, 'Good morning, m'Lady'. An hour or two earlier we had all breakfasted together!

Betting shops became legal in 1961. Here punters study the form.

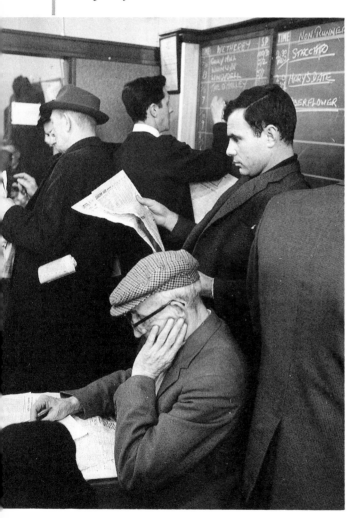

Derby Day, 1987. A bookmaker encouraging punters to place their bets.

Every year the Scotts and the Shepherd-Crosses had a party for their friends in Liverpool at the National Meeting. There was a game of 'chemmy' after dinner – I still have the 'Shoe' filled with the cards we used. There would be perhaps 20 of us sitting round the table, friends dropped in and Archie sat at the head with Peter beside him keeping the book. Archie was in control and his word was law. No one was allowed to get into trouble. It was great fun!

I must mention another side of this remarkable man. On occasions he was known to have helped an unwise punter who was badly in debt to the bookmakers. Quite a few people have Archie to thank for this generosity and help. . .

Having started out with Sidney Fry, Archie went out on his own from 1933, the year Hyperion won the Derby. Then in 1939 he joined Dick Fry for a long and well-known partnership until Dick died in 1960 at the age of ninety-six. They always operated on the rails, where neither umbrellas nor seats were allowed while a race was running, the exception being Mrs Vernet, who used to make a book for Ladbrokes, and she would sit on a box with a rug over her knees.

At the outbreak of war, Archie Scott joined the 6th Battalion, the Green Howards, where he was to prove so calm under duress and such a natural leader of men that, had this been his chosen profession, he could have scaled great heights. Aged over thirty with only his school OTC behind him, Archie nevertheless was promoted to company commander after only a few weeks' training. In April 1940, in France to help build an airfield at Arras, the battalion was caught up in the German breakthrough and forced to help fight a rearguard action, followed by an eighty-mile march to Dunkirk, where Archie showed 'outstanding qualities'.

A contemporary, Sir Richard Sykes, said after his death, 'Disaster seemed imminent every minute of the day and night, but this left him quite undeterred and with his calm temperament and subtle humour, his presence was invaluable to the upkeep of morale under conditions of such adversity.' Archie went on to the Middle East to serve in the Eighth Army, but he contracted rheumatic fever, from which he never fully recovered.

After the war, his business was known as A. C. Scott Ltd and was renowned for a racecourse clientèle of high quality. But times were hard, and in 1960 his company was taken over by Alfred Cope, which was in turn taken over by the Hill Organization eighteen months later. It was during this period that more and more of Archie's energies were channelled into the administrative side of the profession and this was where his education and background were to prove so invaluable.

Much of the 'zing' had gone out of racing for him. 'Racing used to be a sport,' he told a *Sporting Life* reporter in 1963. 'Now it's hard, commercial business. It's not fun any more. Frankly, the past three or four years have been a nightmare.'

The ante-post favourite, Pinturischio, had been 'got at' before the Derby of 1962 and as a result the Jockey Club was introducing stringent identity schemes to tighten up security not only at racecourses but in training yards too. Archie Scott was regularly travelling to Portman Square at the Jockey Club's behest to see how his profession could assist in bringing the dopers to justice. The Jockey Club made no secret of the fact that it believed bookmakers were withholding information; coupled with racing's dire financial difficulties, a Tote monopoly looked more and more on the cards.

Archie Scott worked all through the Macmillan government as chairman of the National Bookmakers' and Associated Bodies' Joint Protection Association, from 1957 to 1964. This was the body whose negotiations with the government resulted in the Betting and Gaming Act of 1960. Archie was asked to advise Home Secretary, Rab Butler, on the opening of betting shops and was in close contact with him and his Under-Secretary, Mr Renton, throughout the period of gestation and legislation, roughly from 1957 until it came into being in 1961.

The offices he held and the committees he served on were impressive, and it was really only those working with him who knew how great his achievements were. Apart from the joint protection association, he was also chairman of the National BPA (later called the National Association of Bookmakers); he was a member of the Pitch Rules and Administrative Committee of the NPBA, playing a leading part in bringing about the introduction of the Ferguson Scheme; he was a director of the Southern BPA; a member of Tattersall's Committee; Chairman of the Association of Rails' Bookmakers; Chairman of the Bookmaker's Betting Levy Committee, and a member of the Peppiatt Committee. His work was regarded as a milestone in the history of bookmaking. He was the first bookmakers' representative to sit on Field Marshal Lord Harding's Betting Levy Board as the bookmaker member when it was formed in 1962. At the time, Archie Scott said, 'It's been seven days a week for me for years.'

For thirty-three years he had one clerk on the rails, such was the loyalty he induced and the respect he commanded; in all that time, they were 'Haining' and 'Mr Scott' to each other, but when introducing him, Archie always referred to 'my colleague, Mr Haining'.

Throughout his unorthodox career, Archie Scott

remained the model of a gentleman, and fairness was one of his trademarks. He hated restrictions on punters, and thought it a disgrace when colleagues gave only one-sixth the odds on each-way betting or even insisted on win only. He deplored the activities of the 'knock-out' people at one particular meeting and refused to make a book there. When it came to people owing him money, he could be very hard on those who *wouldn't* pay, but was consideration itself to someone who couldn't.

In the end, Archie's health failed him; he told his doctor he was too busy (on all the committees) to have a heart operation; he once described his avoidance of a Tote monopoly as 'a desperately close call, a photo finish'.

Archie Scott was only sixty-two when he died after a heart attack in 1965. His war illness, his unstinting work on behalf of his profession and personal tragedy had taken their toll. His wife was killed in a car accident near Newmarket in 1962, and shortly before his own death one of his sons, Ian, was killed on active service in Aden.

After his death, a memorial fund was set up and the Archie Scott Memorial Trophy is now run at Stratford-upon-Avon each November, when the trophy is presented to the winner by his daughter, Fiona Shepherd-Cross, who married James, the son of his lifelong friend.

Tributes came pouring in: Geoffrey Hamlyn of the *Sporting Life* said he 'will go down in history as the man who very nearly brought about unity in the bookmaking industry, a well nigh impossible task; if Archie had never lived, there would probably now be no bookmakers at all, to the great detriment of the racing public . . . but for his efforts there would almost certainly have been a Tote monopoly or worse.'

The late William Hill said bookmakers everywhere owed him a debt of gratitude, and the good things he did on their behalf would live long after him. 'He possessed scrupulous fairness and impartiality, he was the first gentleman of bookmaking; but for his selfless devotion and unswerving loyalty to their cause at a time when far-reaching political decisions were in the balance . . . there might be no bookmakers today.'

He left behind a legend of the sort on which racing thrives.

The Archie Scott Memorial Challenge Cup, which is raced for each November at Stratford-upon-Avon.

Beating the Bookies

Alex Bird, professional punter

Probably the last of the big time professional punters was Alex Bird. He began life as a bookmaker, only to cross to the other side of the rails.

From humble beginnings in a Manchester suburb, Alex Bird was another of those who became hooked on racing as a boy in the 1920s. His father used to beaver away in a little attic room and his mother, who ran a grocery, was very cagey about what he was up to, arousing young Alex's curiosity. When taking up coffee or a message to his father, Alex would try to see what was going on among the pile of papers on the desk before being hustled out of the place. Ostensibly a coal merchant, Mr Bird senior was also a bookmaker.

In time, Alex inveigled his way into being allowed to open the clock bags brought in by a runner who had picked up bets from a local factory; gradually he was allowed to work out the winnings on simple odds, and by using his brain and illustrating his aptitude, he was eventually allowed at fourteen to forgo the offer of a scholarship and enter the business fulltime. But he was not to stay on that side of the game for long. His astute brain realized that there was money to be made in betting as long as he studied the form seriously. Night after night he would sit up late, to the worry of his mother, as he assiduously pored over the form books. Patience and planning, he deduced, were as important as form, jockey, going and distance. In betting, he had found his *métier* in life.

Alex Bird's is an intriguing story. Not for him the rich man squandering fortunes in the ring; he never called himself a *gambler* but an investor, something he had to explain to the taxman time and again. He watched, he made notes, he waited. He was not an impulse gambler, something that has caused the downfall of so many. His first major run of successes came with what he called his 'thieving' bets. He discovered that when there

Professional punter Alex Bird.

was an odds-on favourite, a near foolproof way of making money was to back the second favourite each way.

Before long, Alex learned that there is no such thing as earning easy money from the bookies: not because he started losing, but because by conti-

nual winning, bookies simply declined to take further bets from him. He started opening accounts with bookies who advertised in the press. They would take up to four telegrammed bets from one post office. Alex would write out the telegrams in readiness all bar the name of the horse, wait for the first indication of prices to appear on his father's tapes, fill in his selection, then snatch his bike and cycle furiously to the post office to despatch them.

His system proved too good and the bookies once more closed in on him, either restricting his betting or closing his accounts altogether. So, still a teenager, he began to employ commissioning agents, as big gamblers had been doing for two centuries. Anyone who thinks backing horses is a simple matter of handing over the money soon learns otherwise. The whole thing becomes a game of cat and mouse, of 'beating the bookies'.

By the 1960s Alex would regularly change both methods and agents in a bid to confuse the bookies. When betting shops became legal in 1961, he used twelve men and six cars in a foolproof method. The shops had to inform their HQ of any bets of £5 or more before accepting them. Alex's men put on £4 15s a time, and each man would reach up to seventy shops from the time they opened at 9 a.m. until the off. Alex himself would often stay away from the course when he had a runner of his own to stop bookies thinking he fancied it. Of course, a lot depended on the discretion of his helpers in holding their tongues; all this, just to put on £2000!

Alex Bird was nineteen years old when a bookie first defaulted on him, a dispiriting experience; conversely, when Littlewoods once sent him a cheque for £25 in error, he returned it to them – and years later, that remained the only firm never to close or restrict his betting.

He learned the folly of betting on handicaps, the more so after the introduction of computer handicapping, eliminating the human margin of error. He never backs in them. Instead, he worked out his amazing photo-finish theory, and for years he reaped rich rewards from it. It was in 1948 that he first discovered a sort of optical illusion applied to photo finishes. Almost invariably, it was the horse on the *far* side which looked as it if had won, and bookies would accordingly lay more attractive odds on the other; yet often it was the nearside horse that won.

Alex stood himself by the post to discover why. He closed his left eye and he kept his head still instead of moving it with the horses (much as spectators follow the ball in a tennis match). That way, he could see which horse had really won. The method proved so infallible that he won 500 *consecutive* photo-finish bets, at an average of £500 a time. It was now the 1950s, and his betting turnover was running at £2 million a year. It enabled him to buy a mansion, a plane and a string of racehorses; to keep the best of company; and to have a private dining-room at Aintree and a box at Old Trafford, home of his native Manchester United football team.

One thing he has never cracked, in spite of his bookmaking beginnings, is the bookmakers' 'underworld'. Their intelligence network is enormous, accurate and incredibly fast. Thus has it been since time immemorial, for when the great Cloister, winner of the Grand National in 1893, was taken out of the race in the next two successive years, his odds had mysteriously lengthened virtually before the trainer himself knew there was anything amiss. The horse's owner, Charles Duff, went to great lengths to avoid skulduggery, employing private security guards and even changing trainers, and it will never be known for sure if the afflictions were genuine mishaps or the result of some low-handed dealings. Whichever, the bookies' underground information network knew, and this in the days when the telephone was in its infancy and long before fast cars, let along fax machines and the like.

In 1952 camera timing became available on a number of courses, so Alex Bird was able to do his homework even more precisely. He never stopped studying form, timing races himself and finding new outlets for placing bets. The only way to make big money betting, he concluded, was to have nerves of steel and these he possessed in abundance. Not that it was simply steel nerves and rash gambling; every single bet he made was still considered carefully as his computer brain sifted the data he fed into it: the draw, the going, the horse, the previous times, etc.

The one medium through which he did not make much money was his own horses. 'Some stewards never believed I could be so successful betting without being crooked,' he says, 'but in fact I lost money owning horses.' Nevertheless, they were a way of putting something back into

the sport from which he had gained so much, he felt. But in the mid-1960s, having survived the prospect of there being no bookmakers at all at the start of the decade, everything that he enjoyed and his very means of earning a livelihood looked threatened again with the advent of the off-course betting tax.

His annual profits on a £2 million turnover worked out at 1.83 per cent. The new tax, introduced in 1966, was 2½ per cent. Clearly the days of the professional punter were doomed. Needless to say, a self-made man like Alex Bird does not give up that easily. He simply put his brain into overdrive for a bit. By scouring his betting records,

A picture illustrating Alex Bird's photo-finish theory. Usually the far-side horse looks to have won when in reality it is often the nearside horse, as is shown here with Nimbus (centre) winning the 1949 Derby from Amour Drake (right).

he discovered he most often lost on three-year-old maiden races, especially those for fillies only, so, as he had done with handicaps years before, he simply stopped betting on them – and was just able to continue paying his way. His one major handicap exception, incidentally, was the Grand National, often called the greatest gamble of all,

Backing horses professionally earned Alex Bird the good things in life.

but by paying his usual attention to detail beforehand, Alex very seldom lost on it.

Since then, he has seen the tax increased to its current level of 10 per cent. Although Alex Bird, who refers to bookies as 'my friend the enemy', has obviously *enjoyed* his chosen profession, he does have harsh words for some bookmakers' practices, notably those of 'knocking-in' prices and cramping place odds.

Knocking-in is the technique of forcing artificially short odds at the last minute, so that the starting-price returned is not really true, but it benefits the betting shops offering starting prices. 'It is the equivalent of bookies putting their hands in punters' pockets,' he said, adding that book-

maker John Banks tried to stop it. One devious use is when a horse is obviously about to be withdrawn from a race, not under starter's orders – say, because it has gone lame. The bookies then quickly bring his price to below 10–1 if it was at longer odds and then, although bets on that horse would be void, the bookies are entitled to deduct 10 per cent from the winner's price because the odds of the withdrawn horse had been below 10–1. 'In other words, daylight robbery,' says Alex Bird.

Sixty Years in Racing

Geoffrey Hamlyn, Starting Price reporter

Archie Scott and Alex Bird each represent a different side of betting, but a man with an impartial view of both is Geoffrey Hamlyn, whose sixty years in racing as a Starting Price reporter came about by chance and not, for him, through any boyhood love affair with the sport.

Born at Wandsworth Common in 1910 and educated at Dulwich College, London – 'more a games school than a sports one' – thoughts of racing never entered his head. Instead, when he left school he joined the bank of Thomas Cook and Sons for the princely sum of 37s 6d a week for hours of 9 a.m. to 7 p.m. After three months of abject misery, he jumped at whatever chance his father would offer him.

Mr Hamlyn senior ran a newspaper called

Geoffrey Hamlyn presents his trophy to Countess Marianne Esterhazy at Kempton Park.

Sporting Chat and various tipping agencies. In October 1928 the eighteen-year-old Geoffrey started work for his paper by attending Newmarket. 'His must have been quite a successful publication,' Geoffrey recalls, 'because he educated five of his eight children at public school on it; the other three died.'

Five years later Geoffrey joined the staff of the *Sporting Life*, at the start of a fifty-five-year association with them. 'It was just a job,' he recalls. 'Unemployment was rife and I was glad of anything.' Before long he was embroiled in the sport that was to be his lifelong business. In 1988, at the age of seventy-eight, he was still working part-time for the *Sporting Life* and as Public Relations Officer for bookmaker Victor Chandler. In the thirteen years since his official retirement he spent the first five with Racecourse Security Services, until he was obliged to retire again. But, with a non-inflation-linked pension from the *Life*, he was soon at work again, this time with Ward-Hill for another six years. Although the income was welcome, so was the continued involvement with a craft that played an important part in the everyday life of racing.

It is the role of two independent reporters at each race meeting (four at the big ones like Royal Ascot) to note down the opening prices of every horse in a race and their market movements right up until the off. The two then meet to compare notes and if one, for instance, has seen a horse start at 3–1 and the other only saw 4–1, they compromise and return it as 7–2. Then, until the 1980s, they immediately gave their return to Extel to wire around the country, a job that is now performed by Satellite Information Services. This service, started in May 1987, televises two race meetings a day to those who can receive it with full betting information.

The starting-price method was devised in 1926, but its history dates back much further to when, in the 1850s, bookmakers used to congregate at Hyde Park on race days and undercover wagering took place – until the police put a stop to it. The layers then went to ground in clubs and dens in the Strand and Fleet Street. Firms advertising that they were members of Tattersall's and Newmarket Rooms told their clients that all wagers would be settled by the returns published in *Bell's Life*. In

The name of the 1861 Derby winner Kettledrum is posted outside the office of Bell's Life, *the forerunner of the* Sporting Life.

Among the lady owners of the 1930s were the big punters Dorothy Paget and Mrs J.V. Rank.

1859 the sporting papers *Bell's Life* and *Bell's Life in London* went to court over the similarity in their names and as a result *Bell's Life* became the *Sporting Life*.

After the First World War, the *Sporting Life*, *Bell's Life in London* and the *Sportsman* amalgamated, leaving the *Sporting Chronicle* as the only other paper publishing starting-prices. (That paper folded in 1985, but the *Racing Post*, founded by the Maktoum brothers, was launched in 1986.) In 1926, rather than have different starting-prices printed, the *Life* and *Chronicle* agreed to get together to produce a composite return, a practice which survived even the *Chronicle*'s demise, with some of their staff retained expressly for the purpose.

It was to the long since defunct pony racing at Northolt, buried under a housing estate after the Second World War, that Geoffrey Hamlyn was first despatched by the *Life*. He remembers it as way ahead of its time, 'in my opinion the best model of a racecourse this country has produced from a spectator's point of view'. It had all the facilities that many of the stands built in the 1960s were just beginning to incorporate, such as lifts, and there was catering of a high standard with low prices. It was the first place to stage evening racing and during the summer several members would go racing in evening dress.

It was also the 'nursery' ground of several men who later became prominent flat trainers, such as Bill Wightman, and the betting market there was stronger than at many flat-race meetings today. It also attracted some big gamblers, not least the eccentric owner Dorothy Paget.

After six years on the Army staff in the war (the only time in his life he has ever driven a car),

Geoffrey Hamlyn returned to the *Life*, covering meetings all over the Midlands and North, and became chief Starting Price reporter. There are only two race meetings in England he has not been to – Hexham and Cartmel – and to every one of them he chose to travel by train. He made an unusual figure, neat bowler hat and brolly by his side, as he sat, back to engine, corridor side, neatly entering the names of every horse engaged that day in his notebook. This he kept cleanly wrapped in a copy of the *Financial Times*, 'because its black print does not come off like other papers'.

Until after the war, there was enormous English wealth in racing. 'Since then I have seen unbelievable changes,' said Geoffrey Hamlyn, speaking in 1988.

There have been more changes in racing in the last thirty years than in the previous 300, especially in betting, in bloodstock values and, in particular, in the *type* of owners.

When I started, there were at least a dozen dukes racing, and I can't think of any now, except Roxburghe. Even the present Duke of Norfolk doesn't race. Now it is businessmen who are taking to it, not because they know anything about it but because they want to increase their firm's prestige, and they sponsor races.

Like almost everyone else in racing, he has nothing but good to say of the influx of Arab

owners – 'although I wish there weren't quite so many horses named in an Arab way because in ten years there won't be an English name among us'. He adds, 'They behave in the most admirable fashion, and they put massive fortunes into the game.'

He has also seen enormous changes in the bookmaking fraternity and betting in general.

The whole concept of bookmaking was changed with the introduction of the Betting Levy in 1961–62. In 1961 all the quality press came down in favour of a Tote monopoly, but Peter O'Sullevan was one who said he might never go racing again; racing would be as dull as ditchwater. Bookmakers have Archie Scott to thank for still being in existence; he came the closest to anyone of uniting bookmakers, all off his own bat, but they have reverted to pursuing their own interests and are not united today.

Hamlyn feels the Tote has certain inestimable advantages:

The Tote takes out 25–28 per cent – what bookie wouldn't rejoice to win 28 per cent on each race every day! They would think it was heaven on earth. The Tote has a far better deal. It has all the best pitches on the racecourse – they are to be found everywhere, in the members' bars, function rooms and so forth.

At Goodwood, the new stand allows Tote only, although Ascot allows both; Newbury didn't allow bookies in the members' enclosure at all until well after the war. Then, there was a racing boom for ten to twelve years, but after that the industry became so hard up that when the Levy came in, it was glad to have the bookies' money. The Levy was like manna from heaven for racing.

He adds:

One reads today in the sporting press of horses being backed to win five, ten or twenty thousand pounds, but in terms of fifty years ago, when these sums were wagered every day of the week, one comes to realize that the only really successful punter today is the Government, which 'wins' around £300 million, year after year, from the followers of the sport of kings.

Although there is still some anti-bookie prejudice, their social status has changed a great deal.

Before the war, it would have been unthinkable for a bookmaker to have been to public school (Archie Scott was the exception, of course) but now it is not rare and Victor Chandler, for example, attended the country's most expensive one, Millfield.

Bookmakers, like so many others in racing, have their family dynasties. Chandler's, for instance, was founded by Victor's grandfather; he had eight children and all seven sons went into either bookmaking or greyhound racing. Victor himself planned to go into the hotel business, but when his father died at an early age, he took to the business like the proverbial duck to water, and today he is known for laying the biggest bets of anyone on the racecourse.

The Stein's were another great bookmaking family, with four brothers, Harry, Maxsie, Jack and Isaac (Ike); Harry – 'Snouty' – revolutionized betting on the rails before the war, starting in 1936. He was the leader of the ring from 1936 until his death in 1945. His empire went to Max Parker, who bought Ladbrokes in 1957 for surely one of the greatest bargains ever, at about £¼ million. Jack Stein, the father of Cyril, was a quiet man, unlike the others, and ran the blower service for the brothers.

Of William Hill, Geoffrey Hamlyn says simply:

He was the greatest racecourse bookmaker there has ever been or is ever likely to be; he came to the front between 1941 and 1955, and was the right man in the right place at the right time; all the money was there, the war was over, there were no off-course betting shops, televised racing or tax and everyone flocked to the racecourse, with black marketeers spending their ill-gotten gains and people just out of the services getting rid of their gratuities as fast as they could.

He deserved his success, in Hamlyn's view. He was invariably first to call the prices, running down the card, giving a price for every horse again and again. Other bookmakers would watch him and follow his lead. At Royal Ascot he would take £20,000 *minimum* per race (the equivalent of £200,000 plus today).

The biggest gamble he took in his life was in the 1947 Derby, for which Tudor Minstrel was the red-hot favourite. Trained by Fred Darling, who sent out a total of seven Derby winners from his

William Hill, 'monarch of the ring'.

Tudor Minstrel, the biggest Derby gamble of all time.

Beckhampton stable, a record jointly held with Robert Robson and John Porter, he was unbeaten as a two-year-old, then won the 2000 Guineas with contemptuous ease, ridden by Gordon Richards. Tudor Minstrel was acclaimed 'Horse of the Century' and money poured in on him for the Derby. But William Hill was convinced Epsom would not suit the horse and laid fearlessly against him. He stood to lose £175,000 (the equivalent of £2 million today), but Tudor Minstrel finished fourth. Hamlyn rates this the biggest Derby gamble of all time, with that of Dancing Brave, who also failed (in 1986) the next.

'William Hill was the monarch of the ring,' says Geoffrey Hamlyn. 'He could be volatile one minute and charming the next; he could be stubborn and would never admit to being wrong. You could admire him but it was hard to love him.' William Hill's career ended in typical style, when, during the Royal Ascot meeting of 1955, a fellow layer refused to take a £3000 to £1000 bet. Hill stood down there and then, never to return.

Geoffrey recalls his meeting in 1936 at Northolt with the man who revolutionized betting in Australia, Robert Sievier, who was one of England's most prolific gamblers and prominent owners. It was he who owned and trained the mighty Sceptre, sometimes acclaimed the greatest filly of all time, the horse who came the nearest of any in history to winning all five classics, failing only in the Derby of 1902. Had she been trained by a professional then, as she was to be later by Alec Taylor at Manton after Sievier had to sell her to

Robert Sievier, one of England's most prolific gamblers, was responsible for revolutionizing betting in Australia towards the end of the last century.

meet some of his debts, she might well have set that record.

It was in 1886 that Sievier took the Australian betting world by storm. The practice there at that time was to bet only on double events and every layer was his own clerk. He would generally offer to bet on 'this and the next'. So even if his first horse won, a punter would lose if his second did not. What is more, no one was paid until settling day. Sievier recalled in his memoirs:

When, therefore, I took up my position on the Adelaide Racecourse with a clerk by my side, I created no little excitement, and when I gave out that I would pay on every race immediately after the winner had weighed in, and that my transactions would be confined to single and not double events, the fraternity looked on me in wonderment, mingled with despair, while the public came up smiling and I did a roaring trade.

My first venture showed a profit of more than £1500 at the end of the day and it was telegraphed to all the newspapers that a prominent English bookmaker had arrived from Tattersall's in England and had paralysed betting in South Australia!

Of pre-Second World War gamblers in Britain, Miss Dorothy Paget's tilts at the ring were legendary, and she remains the only owner in history to win the Derby (with Straight Deal), the Grand National (with Golden Miller), seven Cheltenham Gold Cups (five with Golden Miller, one each with Roman Hackle and Mont Tremblant) and the Champion Hurdle four times (twice with Insurance, once each with Solford and Distel).

Geoffrey Hamlyn, who knew her secretary and introduced her to one or two bookmakers on Miss Paget's behalf, says:

It is impossible to overestimate the influence she exercised on jump racing; it is no exaggeration at all to say she transformed it.

When she bought Golden Miller and Insurance for modest sums in 1931, her success was immediate and sustained and caught the public imagination to an extent that had never occurred before.

Her betting was eccentric, as she was herself, but although she sometimes won huge sums, the bookmakers generally took it in good part because she often lost more. At the outbreak of the Second World War, she and another woman, Mrs J. V. Rank, were the biggest punters in the ring, thinking nothing of wagering £10,000 on their horses. While bookmakers will not always accept such sums from professionals, they will accept the 'mug punters' bets with alacrity.

Golden Miller met far stronger opposition than Arkle ever did, says Geoffrey Hamlyn, 'but he had the good sense to hate Aintree'.

The Hon. Dorothy Paget with her champion, Golden Miller. She spent huge sums on bloodstock, not always with adequate returns, but Golden Miller made up for her many disappointments.

Britain's biggest betting day, when housewives and businessmen alike have a flutter on the Grand National. No matter how good the TV coverage, nothing beats the atmosphere at Aintree.

It is difficult for a dishonest bookmaker to exist today; indeed, if he does not fulfil a betting obligation by a Monday, he can be 'struck off' on the Tuesday by Tattersall's Committee, which is the profession's ruling body and watchdog. 'Yet a punter can owe a bookie a fortune, and have no intention of paying,' points out Geoffrey Hamlyn. However, he can be called before Tattersall's Committee and ordered to pay so much a week, much as fines can be dealt with in court.

Discussing modern developments in betting, Geoffrey Hamlyn, perhaps understandably conservative, still believes the Racecourse Association was wrong to let Satellite Information Services take on the role of Extel 'shows', results, etc.

Extel had produced a perfectly adequate system for donkey's years. SIS have got something to offer, and racing may benefit in the long term; if you go into betting shops now there are the TV screens, and it helps journalists to have it in the press room at race meetings, and for trainers at home. But it is not yet shown in parts of the London area because the satellite dishes have to be put up with the owner's consent, and often it is difficult to locate the freehold owners.

But whether it is a good thing to let the Big Three – Ladbrokes, Corals and Hills/Mecca – run the thing, I don't know, although they are very efficient, and a vast sum of money, £25 million in five years, has been promised to racecourses.

It sounds a little bit like manna from heaven all over again somehow.

A modern-day betting shop with its extensive facilities, including satellite screens.

'Arise, Sir Gordon'

Gordon Richards, 1904-86

On 3 October 1933 Gordon Richards rode the last winner at Nottingham and went through the card the following day at Chepstow with another six winners. He then had a ride in every race at Chepstow the day after. Rugby schoolboy David Swannell relayed the results as they came through his headphones, and the clients who had crowded into his study heard history made. By the end of racing on 5 October Gordon had ridden twelve consecutive winners and was beaten by a neck and a head on the thirteenth and most fancied ride.

By the end of the season he had ridden 259 winners, having passed, at Liverpool on 8 November, the record set up by Fred Archer forty-eight years

earlier and, by an extraordinary coincidence, on the exact anniversary of his death. At a prep school in Norfolk, one nine-year-old pupil, John Tosetti, was singled out by the press for an interview. What did he think, now that the record of his grandfather, Fred Archer, had been beaten?

The grey-bearded, retired wine merchant has inherited his grandfather's height and bearing. The only outward sign of any racing connection at his tiny bungalow in the Buckinghamshire village of Adstock, home of bloodstock agent and stud-owner James Delahooke, is a picture of Fred Archer and two racing plates on his house sign. Inside, there are one or two nice pictures and a

Gordon Richards delicately poised, his expressive face showing a combination of concentration and anticipation, his whip held lightly in his hand, as he reaches his 100th winner of the 1945 season.

couple of Fred's whips, one of them most delicate, but much of the memorabilia has already been donated to the National Horseracing Museum at Newmarket. One item reached there by a roundabout route: John Tosetti donated Fred Archer's racing bag to an auction in aid of the worthwhile charity, the Injured Jockeys' Fund. He thought it might make about £50 and helped the bidding along in the early stages. Then it soared, the hammer finally coming down at £500. The purchaser was TV racing commentator and former amateur rider Brough Scott, now editorial director of the *Racing Post*, who immediately donated his acquisition to the museum.

The schoolboy passion for racing, meanwhile, never deserted David Swannell, who went on to become a respected Jockey Club handicapper and later a trustee of the National Horseracing Museum. Not unnaturally, he idolized Gordon Richards, who could, he says, have gone to the top in any chosen sphere.

> He was one of the most attractive characters I have ever met, the kindest and best tempered of men. Not that he would stand any nonsense – you couldn't take liberties with him.
>
> But I never heard him say anything against anyone, and I never heard a cross word against him; nobody did more good for racing. He had a ready wit but was modest with it.

Gordon Richards did not have a racing background: his father was a miner in Shropshire. His first dealings with racing were somewhat startling, for he was apprenticed to Irishman Paddy Hartigan, who, like many in the 1920s, liked nothing more than a rousting party in the Adelphi Hotel, Liverpool, after the Grand National; unfortunately, one year Paddy fell out of a bedroom window and was killed. Gordon's indentures were transferred to Paddy's brother Martin Hartigan, one of whose owners was Jimmy White, a tremendous gambler who won a fortune and lost it all. It was for him that Gordon rode his first winner, and soon he became a 'boy wonder'.

The idol on whom Gordon modelled himself, and before long superseded, was Steve Donoghue, he of 'Come on, Steve!' fame who was particularly associated with the great stayer, Brown Jack.

Gordon Richards was a short-legged, small man, so wasting was not the problem for him that it was for Archer and Piggott. He had tremendous strength and balance in the saddle, and this was probably the secret of his success, coupled with his 'thinking' brain.

It was in 1930 that he rode his first of fourteen classic winners, Rose of England, for trainer Captain Hogg in the Oaks. Soon afterwards he began his long and faithful association with Fred Darling at Beckhampton, the splendid Wiltshire stables that began life as a coaching inn, when the first publican doubled as a racehorse trainer, and retain much of the original charm in the hands of present incumbent Jeremy Tree. Here Gordon Richards became a legend in his own lifetime and his loyalty to his owners was an example that many since would have done well to follow.

In terms of sheer record, his is the greatest of all. Today, in spite of modern transport and an increase in meetings, no other jockey has topped 200 winners in a season, yet Gordon Richards surpassed this tally twelve times. In the 1947 season he rode 269 winners. He first became champion jockey in 1925, and took the title a staggering twenty-six times in total – this at a time when there were many able jockeys riding and apprentices were given a thorough grounding in terms of time, trouble and attention. The nearest anyone had ever come to this record was George Fordham, who between 1855 and 1871 was champion jockey fourteen times.

With all this success, however, the most important race of all, the Derby, kept eluding Gordon. It was with a certain ironic twist that just after being knighted by the Queen, he at last won the Derby, beating the Queen's horse! It was 1953, one year before Sir Gordon retired following a bad fall, that his mount Pinza, owned by Sir Victor Sassoon, ran clean away from the Queen's Aureole in the closing stages.

Sir Gordon trained for a while and then became racing manager to Lady Beaverbrook. He died in 1986, at the age of eighty-two.

OPPOSITE

Top *Towards the end of his successful career, Gordon Richards at last wins the elusive Derby on Pinza in 1953.*

Bottom left *It was the Queen's horse Aureole that he beat. Here they have a pre-race chat.*

Bottom right *Gordon Richards, knighted in 1953, took up training on retiring from the saddle.*

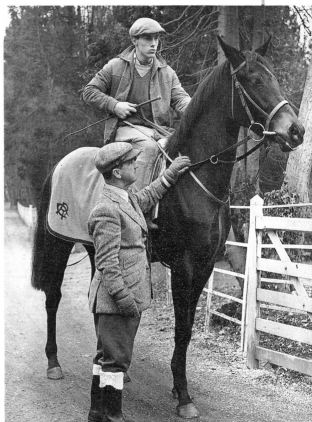

Of Tradition, Triumph and Tragedy
Golden Miller and the Grand National

It is early morning, but sleep has been difficult, with nerves pounding and interruptions in the yard outside frequent. There must have been a late arrival. Ossie Dale, the stable manager, was there as ever to greet them and allocate the horse a stable. Would it be one whose door bears the name of a past Grand National winner or more? The girl shifted uneasily in the makeshift bed again; the lads' and the girls' dormitories had been full when she arrived, and a camp bed in the office would have to do. How would her horse do tomorrow? Hers, in that she tended it, groomed

Early morning exercise on the course is part of Grand National tradition.

Trainer Fred Winter, who won the National twice as a jockey and twice as a trainer, watches attentively.

Members of the public walk round the course escorted by Bob Champion (red) and Graham McCourt (yellow).

it, exercised it, cleaned out its stable and was the one who knew it as an individual.

By six in the morning, relieved to have something to do beyond tossing, she was out and saddling him up. The dull early-morning mist could have been radiant sunshine if the prevailing atmosphere was anything to go by. There's the favourite; oh, there's old so and so; I wonder if he'll get beyond Becher's this year; here comes that wily trainer, he'll exercise away from the waiting watchers for sure; and there's the leading jump jockey; will he break his jinx in the mighty race this year?

The pre-breakfast exercise, or 'nose blow' for the contestants, has become part of the Grand National ritual, with ordinary, eager members of the public who are willing to get up early out on the course alongside famous trainers and the inevitable press corps, watching the runners and their jockeys acquaint themselves and have a leg stretch. Afterwards, there are hot bacon butties and steaming coffees out of plastic mugs.

There is time during the morning for a walk round the course, guided by an expert who has done it for himself, so the crowds can see at close

hand the actual size of the awesome fences, and be told how they are built, and at which ones famous horses have come unstuck.

That evening, as the last of the beer drinkers has gone home and the papers have already printed several issues with all the dramatic details of the race, the place is deserted, save for a sea of litter strewn across the grandstands, the lawns and even the course itself.

This is Grand National Day, and after more than one and a half centuries there is still the same eager anticipation there was on that bright February day in 1839 when the entrepreneurial hotelier William Lynn got the great race off the ground in front of a crowd so huge that it is nearly unimaginable in the pre-motorized transport and pre-television and radio build-up days.

Since then the Grand National has had a greater following than any other race in the world; even during periods in the doldrums, when rival sponsored, televised races offered near parity prize

A team of course builders put the finishing touches to Becher's Brook.

money with half the risk and the Cheltenham Gold Cup took over the mantle of most important steeplechase; even during disputes and doubts about its survival, when owner Mrs Mirabel Topham determined to sell it for building development, in spite of a covenant by Lord Sefton, from whom her family bought the course in 1949, restricting it to racing or agricultural purposes only – a deed that was twice upheld in law only to be overturned finally in Mrs Topham's favour; always the fascination has remained. It could be called the race that refuses to die, and it is one that from the start held the public imagination. It was certainly with the public's help that enough money was raised to buy the course from property developer Bill Davis and the race was finally saved for posterity.

The purchase price was £3.4 million, of which approximately £2 million was raised by public donation, £1 million was loaned by the Levy Board, and £½ million was given by the current sponsors, Seagram. On purchase, the trustees granted a 999-year lease to Aintree Racecourse Co. Ltd, which is a subsidiary company of the Jockey Club.

When the appropriately named Lottery won its first running, the horses had to contend with much plough and some dirty tricks (one horse was 'kidnapped' in running by the mob to prevent it from winning), and although it had the fence and brook into which Captain Becher fell, thus immortalizing them, and a huge wall in front of the stands, most of the fences were very small. The wall did not survive many years and by the end of the nineteenth century, following complaints from the National Hunt Committee to the race organizers, Messrs Tophams, that too many people were dangerously crowding the horses at fences, the course was railed in, and the fences took on the uniform appearance of today, although the last piece of cultivated land was not done away with until 1951.

The birth of steeplechasing itself goes back much further, to County Cork, Ireland, when in 1752 two celebrated gentlemen, Mr Cornelious O'Callaghan and Mr Edmund Blake, matched their hunters over the four and a half miles of country between the churches at Buttevant and St Leger, Doneraile, or in other words, from steeple to steeple. It was nearly 100 years before steeplechasing began to take place in a more organized, formal fashion, when in 1830 one Thomas Coleman, landlord of the Turf Hotel at St Albans, laid out a circular steeplechase course, thus aiding visibility enormously for the spectators. It was an immediate success, and by 1842 there were sixty-six steeplechase courses in England, the most important being at Cheltenham, Aintree and Aylesbury. At the start of the twentieth century, there were 131 tracks in total, a number which has now declined to fifty-nine.

Until the Second World War, the Grand National was the premier steeplechase, and even since

Rounding up loose horses in the car park after the 1982 Grand National.

No Grand National partnership better sums up the triumphs of the race than that of Bob Champion and Aldaniti, winners in 1981.

then, none of the romance or fairy-tale element has been lost. Who could forget Crisp's gallant defeat in 1973? Or the record-breaking three wins and two seconds of Red Rum? Or the magic win of cancer-sufferer Bob Champion on the 'leggy' Aldaniti in 1981? Or how Foinavon's 100–1 (444–1 on the Tote) win served as a reminder of the lottery of the race in 1967, when he alone avoided the big pile-up at the twenty-third fence at the first attempt? To say nothing of the heartbreak of

OPPOSITE
Top *On his way to an historic third victory, Red Rum clears Becher's Brook in the Grand National of 1977.*

Bottom *Eleven years later, as part of the race's 150th anniversary celebrations, Red Rum was present at the unveiling of his statue by the Princess Royal.*

seeing the Queen Mother's Devon Loch fall on the flat within yards of the winning-post in 1956.

All these stories were simply part of the race's tradition: a tiny grey horse, so lovable that he was christened The Lamb, won it twice, once after a vivid dream from his owner that he would do so; two weedy chestnut full-sisters, cast-offs from the flat, Emblem and Emblematic, who gave George Stevens two of his record five riding wins in the race; and the magnificent Manifesto, runner eight times, winner twice and third three times through the turn of the century. Then there was Moifaa, reputedly shipwrecked on his voyage over from New Zealand, and, of course, the mighty Golden Miller.

A dominant and domineering woman, Mrs Mirabel Topham ruled over Aintree for years. She always thought she knew best. In 1952, for example, she insisted on providing a private radio commentary following a dispute over copyright with the BBC (she was for ever trying to increase her revenue from them). The result was such a shambles that she felt obliged to hand the job back to the

professionals the next year. But in the 1960s she would not give in so easily and was determined to sell Aintree for property development. Thus began the string of 'last' Grand Nationals, before the race was finally rescued in 1983.

Another woman who was to dominate National Hunt racing, possibly with even greater impact, was the Hon. Dorothy Paget. She was leading National Hunt owner in the 1951–52 season with fifty winners, the highest post-war number. She is best remembered for her association with the wonderful chaser Golden Miller.

Born in Ireland, a bay with a white star, by Goldcourt out of Miller's Pride, he developed into as fine a stamp as can be imagined, really standing over some ground, his sensible head set off by an elegant long neck. He was bought by a Northamptonshire dealer, Captain Dick Farmer, for 500 guineas when still overgrown and unfurnished, and was passed on to trainer Basil Briscoe, who is reputed to have said, 'It's a likely chaser I want, not a three-year-old carthorse.' Briscoe had owned two of Golden Miller's older half-brothers and had won races on one of them himself, but even so 'The Miller' surprised everyone when he won two races. By this time he had been bought by stockbroker Philip Carr, whose son, A. W. Carr, captained the English cricket team in 1926, for £1000. He died soon afterwards, and this was when Dorothy Paget entered the story. Briscoe told her he had two horses for her, between them the country's best chaser and best hurdler. What a boast! The Miller, who was to win five Gold Cups and a National, and Insurance, who won two Champion Hurdles, cost Miss Paget £10,000 the pair.

Racing's mixed bag produces all sorts, and Miss Paget was surely the most eccentric of all time. A daughter of Lord Queensborough, she thought nothing of wagers that by today's standards would be simply staggering. She had a penchant for meals at night, employing at her home in Chalfont

OPPOSITE

Top *Carnage at the 23rd fence in 1967 when only Foinavon survived the massive pile-up at the first attempt.*

Bottom *The biggest Grand National mystery of all time: the inexplicable collapse on the run-in of the Queen Mother's Devon Loch in 1956.*

St Giles a night cook who was usually ordered to serve fish and chips; thought nothing of ringing up her trainers in the middle of the night; refused to have anything to do with men if she could possibly avoid it (it is said that Golden Miller was the only male to whom she ever showed any outward affection); was overweight and took no effort with her appearance whatsoever, a battered beret and shabby old coat being her hallmark. She was used to summoning servants to do as she bid and to spending money at her whim (often to the benefit of racing), but one wonders if she was really happy. Although difficult to get to know, she became very much a part of the English racing scene and as such was looked upon quite affectionately.

Basil Briscoe was a complete contrast to her. Educated at Eton and Cambridge, he was always immaculately turned-out and spared no detail in training his horses, being highly strung and a perfectionist. This was ultimately to be his undoing. To begin with, all went well in his association with Miss Paget. Golden Miller, with only four chases behind him, three of them wins, won the Gold Cup of 1932 as a five-year-old. The race itself was still less than a decade old and had not yet usurped the National in esteem, the prize money reflecting that difference: in 1933, the Gold Cup was worth £670 and the National £7345. In 1989 they were worth £61,960 and £68,740 respectively.

When Golden Miller went to Liverpool for his first tilt on the 1933 National as a six-year-old, he was unbeaten in his previous five races that season, including the Gold Cup. From the start, Golden Miller was not a 'natural' Aintree horse, and after he fell on the second circuit (the only time he was ever on the floor in his career) his rider Ted Leader predicted he would never cope with the fences.

The following year, Gerry Wilson had taken over as Golden Miller's rider, and he won his third Gold Cup before again setting sail for Aintree. It was a truly top-class line-up, with the 1929 winner, Gregalach carrying 12 stone 7 pounds, Thomond II on 12 stone 4 pounds, Golden Miller on 12 stone 2 pounds and Delaneige on 11 stone 6 pounds. Top weight today has to be 'not less than 11 stone 10 pounds', and a few years ago Burrough Hill Lad was allotted 12 stone 5 pounds, although he did not run.

Golden Miller did not start favourite but his class and courage told, his only mistakes being at Becher's each time. Delaneige, in his element, tried to make all and was still leading four fences from home, but Golden Miller, Forbra and Thomond were close on his heels; the favourite, Really True, had fallen shortly before when going well. Delaneige still just led at the last, but Gerry Wilson simply had to press the button on Golden Miller. He swept into the lead at the last fence and beat Delaneige and Thomond, in a new record time only one year after the last one had been set by Kellsboro' Jack. It was an outstanding victory that stamped Golden Miller one of the greatest steeplechasers of all time, the first horse to complete the Gold Cup/National double, only repeated by L'Escargot since, but not in the same season.

The exploits of Golden Miller the following year, 1935, were sensational. Believing nothing of note would oppose him in the Gold Cup, Basil Briscoe had been relatively light on the horse's preparation, aiming to have him at his peak for the tilt at a second Grand National success.

Crowds flock round the 1934 winner Golden Miller, ridden by Gerry Wilson and led in by his owner, the Hon. Dorothy Paget.

The Gold Cup, however, turned into one of the greatest steeplechase duels of all time, between Golden Miller and his old rival, Thomond II. Their three rivals, Southern Hero, Avenger and Kellsboro' Jack, were useful horses too, and a huge crowd turned out to watch. They were not to be disappointed.

From the start the race was run at a great gallop on the fast ground, and with a mile to go all five still looked in with a chance. Cresting the top of the hill, with three fences and the long sweep home to come, it lay between Golden Miller and Thomond. The pair were neck and neck and so they remained, a ding-dong battle fencing fast and bravely. Together they landed over the last to face the final, stamina-sapping hill to the cheering crowds. With barely 100 yards to go, Golden Miller found that little bit extra to beat his rival by three-quarters of a length, in a time that eclipsed Easter Hero's record by a full twenty-seven seconds.

It had been a desperately hard race and the Grand National was only fifteen days away. Even so, his adoring public would not hear of defeat for The Miller, and backed him down to an incredible 2–1 favourite for the Grand National. He was to carry 12 stone 7 pounds; the firm ground was against him (although deep mud would not have helped him with his weight burden); and to cap it all, rumours were rife that all was not well with the horse. It was just the sort of tension that did not help Basil Briscoe's easily frayed nerves.

Nightmare became reality in the race, for on the far side on the first circuit, at the open ditch two fences after Valentine's, Golden Miller 'froze' – some said he tried to refuse – and Gerry Wilson was shot off. Dorothy Paget did not take the mishap with good grace, and when she accepted Gerry Wilson's story that the horse had never felt himself in the race, Basil Briscoe took this as a slight on his training. To compound matters, poor Golden Miller was started again the next day in the Champion Chase. This time the partnership only lasted as far as the first fence. A public slanging match ensued, the outcome of which was that Basil Briscoe told Dorothy Paget to remove her horses from his yard within one week. Four days later they were gone. Basil Briscoe was never the same again and moved to a smaller yard; after the war he was barely known in racing circles. He died in 1951 at only forty-eight years old.

Golden Miller was never the same again either, but at least he lived to a ripe old age. He moved to the yard of Donald Snow and then to that of Owen Anthony. He won at Newbury with Gerry Wilson again riding him but when, on the same course, he subsequently ran out, Wilson was 'jocked off' and replaced by Evan Williams for the Gold Cup of 1936, which, with no Thomond in the field, he won with much of his old fire.

For the Gold Cup of 1938 (1937 having fallen victim to the weather) Golden Miller conceded victory to the younger Morse Code, but only by two lengths in a memorable last Gold Cup race for him. This time he was ridden by Frenchie Nicholson.

In all, Golden Miller ran in fifty-two races, won twenty-eight of them, was ridden by a total of seventeen different jockeys and lived until he was thirty years old – in terms of human years, much longer than his principal human counterparts: besides Briscoe, Gerry Wilson died in 1959 and Miss Paget herself was only fifty-four when she died in 1960.

Keeping Up with the Chemist

Jockey Club Security

The phone rang unexpectedly and the voice of Peter Smiles, Director of Security for the Jockey Club, asked if we were going to the Tickham Hunt point-to-point at Detling the next day. If so, could we take a horsebox and driver, as it might be necessary to travel some distance with an equine passenger afterwards?

That was it – no clue as to the reason for this strange request, and we certainly knew better than to ask. The Tickham point-to-point is a well-run affair, one of several hundred like it spread all over the country each spring. Its chalk soil on the North Downs ensures rideable ground in even the wettest weather.

As usual there were a good many runners for the restricted open race, most of them unknown quantities. A strapping chestnut called Red Keidi was among the rank outsiders. If connections had had their way and been able to heap on their money, he would probably have started a short-priced favourite. But he had barely walked a circuit of the paddock when Bob Anderson, the Jockey Club's chief investigating officer, stepped forward and asked the handler to bring the horse back out.

There was a 'passport irregularity', the public was informed, when the horse's withdrawal was announced. Unbeknown to them, it was not the usual thing of a 'flu jab that turned out to have been three days late seven years ago, or something similar, but a question of identity. For the 'novice' Red Keidi was a 'ringer', the racing parlance for a switched horse. In reality, he was the former Monica Dickinson- then Ron Atkins-trained chaser My Virginian, whose record included a steeplechase win at Carlisle; hence the cloak and dagger stuff emanating from Portman Square.

With the setting up of Racecourse Security Services (RSS) in 1972, funded by the Levy Board, there was a special department to deal with the

Peter Smiles, Director of Security for the Jockey Club.

whole question of security and the eternal battle against doping. Before that the Jockey Club's Racecourse Personnel Organization was a 'sort of security organization'.

When Brigadier Henry Green retired in 1977, his position as Director of Security was filled by Peter Smiles, a refreshingly young, non-military man, who gained his early experience of racing administration as an assistant stipendiary steward in Australia, in the Northern District Racing Association of Victoria, based at Bendigo. In his security post, he has been both innovative and intuitive in his fight against 'hanky panky' in the sport.

In The Money hurdling. Later connections tried to run him in a point-to-point as Cobbler's March.

In 1986 the Security and Veterinary field forces of RSS came under the direct wing of the Jockey Club and were renamed the Jockey Club Security Department. The laboratory at Newmarket remained under the Levy Board, with the Jockey Club its principal customers, carrying out dope tests and research.

'Ringing', in fact, is a comparatively rare occurrence in racing. On average there is a detected case about every three and a half years: such as Gay Future in 1976, who ran in his own name but had had a useless horse in his place on the gallops; In The Money, who ran as Cobbler's March in 1978; Good Hand, who ran as Flockton Grey in 1983; and in 1987–88 a case from the world of Arab Horse Society racing came to light, which went to court in April 1989. In such instances, the police and Jockey Club Security liaise closely. The criminal side of the proceedings will be dealt with first and then the racing authorities step in, the usual outcome being that the perpetrator(s) are 'warned off'.

Though rare, ringing is a far from new malpractice in racing, and certainly before identification procedures were tightened up in the 1970s it was easier to do. One of the more notorious cases was in the 1884 Derby, which was 'won' by Running Rein, who was in reality the four-year-old Maccabeus. Suspecting that the horse had been dyed, Lord George Bentinck, the turf dictator of the time, personally visited every chemist and hairdresser between the home of the horse's trainer, gambler Goodman Levy, and his London club, which he frequented daily. The sleuthing paid off, for he found a hairdresser in Regent Street who could remember selling a large bottle

The notorious ringer of 1884, Running Rein (above), who 'won' the Derby when in reality he was a four-year-old, a fact that was uncovered due to the diligence of Lord George Bentinck (right).

of dye to a man answering Goodman Levy's description. Nor did he turn out to be the only ringer in the race, for the unfortunate Leander, who broke his leg on Tattenham Corner and had to be put down, was found, when post-mortemed, to be a horse older than was alleged.

Nor was that the only scandal of the Derby that year, for the favourite, Ratan, was doped. He was the form horse but his jockey, Sam Rogers, contrived to have him 'got at' the night before. It was little consolation for the suffering horse or his connections that Rogers was warned off as a result. Ratan was hardly able to raise a gallop and was described thus by the author Sylvanus in *Byelanes and Downs of England*: 'With his coat blue and shivery and standing in fright, he was finally beaten by wretches he could have distanced had not villainy marked him for her own.' The horse's owner, William Crockford, who founded London's gaming club of that name, was said to have died of shock two days later.

It is against doping and the seedier, seemier side of the sport that Jockey Club Security is chiefly employed. In an effort to stamp out 'undesirables', the investigators no longer merely 'count the number of schooling fences or padlocks on the gate' when recommending a new licence-holder. Instead, their antecedents and ability to finance a business are also taken into consideration, and the onus is now more on the applicant to prove that he is of good character. 'In spite of rigorous screening, one or two still slip through the net who are not a credit to their profession,' Peter Smiles confesses frankly. 'But on the whole, things are much better.'

Security now takes on a much higher profile both on and off the racecourse. In 1985 Peter Smiles appointed four betting intelligence officers to advise the Stewards on market fluctuations, and that number was increased to five three years later. Gradually more authority is being exercised over bookmakers.

'80 to 90 per cent of our work is preventative, by maintaining a presence on the racecourse, in the training centres, at the sales and so forth, and as we have the authority to visit unannounced, we act as a deterrent.' Having said that, Peter Smiles stresses that his organization is by no means aggressive – to the law-abiding. Indeed, trainers who have security/doping problems increasingly call his department first instead of last if they are worried. In other words, in addition to being a racing police force they are also a service, and licensed racing personnel are encouraged to use them as an investigative force. Without exception, the senior staff are ex-police officers, mostly with CID experience, who have retired from the force at about fifty years old with about fifteen years of working life still to contribute.

Another malpractice they are always watching for is fixed racing, or for 'activities that might influence the outcome of a race'. The type of race to be wary of is one with a small field at an out-of-the-way place, and here again the betting market acts as a barometer, often enabling the betting intelligence officers to 'read' a race before it has taken place. 'Nine times out of ten horses run true to the market,' says Peter Smiles. 'Nevertheless, it is not easy to detect a deliberate non-tryer.'

It is often felt that malpractice is less frequent in Tote-monopoly countries, but evidence refutes this. Hong Kong, where a £6 million turnover is a common occurrence on any one race during an ordinary eight-race mid-week card (compared with Royal Ascot's boast of turning over £1 million in 1988) had its scandal of races allegedly rigged by jockeys. America suffered some 'horrendous' race-rigging in the late 1970s. One man laid about $100,000 on one race in order to rig the jockeys, but he was apprehended and put in jail for a long time. In France some years ago, where the *Tierce* is the Tote equivalent, some jockeys who attempted to rig races were also jailed. In many of these countries, the horse is merely a number to the punter, whereas in England the horse himself counts for a great deal.

It was just over 100 years ago that English jockeys were banned from owning or having an interest in a racehorse. Charles Wood, considered second only to Fred Archer in his prime, became too fond of money. He was accused of stopping horses, of running a 'jockeys' ring' to deceive owners and trainers, and of rowing in with the bookies for his own profit. He owned several horses, and their running played such 'ducks and drakes' with the form book that in 1887 the Jockey Club, largely because of him, introduced their new rules. A year later, Wood's licence was also withdrawn.

Doping has been the bane of racing down through the ages and today it is a permanent battle to remain no more than one step behind the

chemist. 'Our detection processes are improving all the time,' says Peter Smiles.

It is a costly battle against the chemist and the unscrupulous, who will always cheat somehow, and the menace is always there.

The problem for us is getting the information on the drugs that could be being used; they are getting more and more sophisticated and we are naturally the last people anyone is going to tell.

Surely, in the interest of racing, people like vets would help?

That profession keeps things fairly close to its chest in their duty to confidentiality. Our best help comes from Customs and Excise with information on what is being imported; also there are useful international forums between vets, scientists and so on which are good for exchanging information and views.

There has been a fairly set pattern to doping over

Security guards prevent intruders, even jockeys, from entering racecourse stables. Here Richard Pitman (second from right) awaits his horse.

the years: in the 1960s it was bookmaker-inspired doping gangs who raided trainers' yards to dope to stop. Fairly hefty sentences after convictions at Lewes and Reading Crown Courts effectively stopped that, but not before some horses had been ruined for life. Then in the late 1970s there was the use of anabolic steroids, which built up young horses' physiques abnormally, enabling them to return 'super-equine' performances. There was a major breakthrough in combating that when the RSS laboratory at Newmarket discovered how to detect them.

The scourge of the 1980s has a far more accidental flavour: tiny traces of forbidden substances were too often being found in proprietary brands of horse cubes; when detected, the inno-

cent trainer was not always heavily fined but automatic disqualification of the horse was and still is mandatory.

The 'Mars Bar' case concerned a four-year-old gelding, No Bombs, who won a hurdle at Worcester in April 1979. It was routinely tested and its urine showed the presence of theobromine, for which no explanation could be found by investigators. It was not until trainer M. H. (Peter) Easterby was at Portman Square about to attend the Disciplinary hearing that his wife telephoned to say that it had come to light that very morning that a lad had fed the horse a Mars Bar in the horsebox on the way to the races.

More recently, thanks to Jockey Club influence internationally, admissible threshold levels have been agreed on certain exogenous substances because it has been proved that horses carry a certain level naturally, and the same applies to fodder made entirely of natural ingredients. Probably the most famous case was that of Hill House in 1967, the horse who manufactured his own dope. He was trained by that great maestro and character Ryan Price, one of the finest men across country in the hunting field, and with the sort of spirit that saw him serve as a commando in the Second World War. Hill House won the race that Captain Price made his own, the Schweppes Gold Trophy handicap hurdle at Newbury in February. He had already won it twice with Rosyth and once with Le Vermontois, underlining his stupendous skill as a trainer. As Ryan Price was to say, he was to be penalized for improving a horse and getting it to win races. He was truly a genius with horses, especially with temperamental ones, and Hill House was most certainly that.

Hill House manufactured so much adrenalin in the excitement of racing (or indeed simply from a change of stable, as later tests at Newmarket were to prove) that the 'non-normal nutrient' cortisol was found in his dope test. Ryan Price was hauled before the Stewards and accused of having not run the horse on its true merits in its previous race and of being the trainer of a horse to which a non-normal nutrient had been administered. In an inquiry that was to last a seemingly eternal six months, Ryan Price, his jockey Josh Gifford and stable staff in Sussex were finally fully vindicated. The zeal with which his defence was pursued by one of his owners, Lady Weir, had much influence on the outcome, for it was she who found a cancer research scientist who specialized in the field of cortisol.

Dr G. F. Marrian wrote:

The facts, to the best of my knowledge, are as follows. In man, and in many other animals, cortisone, cortisol and a number of closely related compounds, are normally secreted by the adrenal glands. These compounds, and some of their metabolic products, appear in the urine, and under conditions of stress the amounts of these compounds in the urine are increased.

While it is possible that cortisone and cortisol may not have been identified in horse urine, it is highly probable that they are normally present. Certainly, a number of closely related compounds have been found normally in horse urine.

This was in sharp contrast to the statement issued by the Stewards' Advisory Committee on the sample from Hill House:

The urine sample contained cortisol (Hydrocortisone).

Cortisol was administered to the horse prior to the race, in a dose sufficient to improve racing performance.

Cortisol is not a normal nutrient.

A number of long-needed reforms came about as a result of the Hill House case, not least of which was that legal representatives of an accused person could be present at future inquiries.

General racecourse behaviour also comes under the Security umbrella, although rowdiness and hooliganism no longer count – it is a sad reflection on the late 1980s that as this regrettable national trait began to spread from the confines of the football terraces to other sports, it was felt that the police force should handle this problem, leaving Racecourse Security the time and resources to concentrate on their specialist tasks.

But one piece of rowdyism that they did deal with most successfully was the 'lavatory roll' incident during Troy's Derby of 1979. As the horses streamed round Tattenham Corner, which is in itself the trickiest part of the race, an overexuberant spectator, already considerably the worse for wear through drink, threw a lavatory roll from the top of an open bus into their midst.

It rolled out and wrapped itself round Yves St Martin, rather like the puppy in the television advert but in far more dangerous circumstances. 'Yves had a complete Gallic sense of humour failure,' says Peter Smiles, 'but it was an extremely dangerous incident.'

So how to pinpoint the culprit from among several thousand racegoers on Epsom Downs? The coach from which the loo roll was thrown could be seen clearly on television replays, and on its side was a large advertisement. Peter Smiles contacted the agency responsible for the advert, established to whom the coach belonged, and from there learned who had hired it for the day:

OPPOSITE

A potentially dangerous episode sorted out by Jockey Club Security was the 'loo roll' incident of 1979, the year Troy won the 200th running of the Derby. The unfortunate recipient of the missile was French jockey Yves St Martin.

the London School of Mines, only a brief stroll away from Portman Square. Peter Smiles and Bob Anderson walked over and asked to see the School's social club secretary. They left having made it clear in no uncertain terms that if the perpetrator was not produced within twenty-four hours, the whole coachload would be handed over to the police.

Next day the culprit concerned was duly brought forward. A non-racing person enjoying a day out, he had been paralytic since 8 a.m. on Derby morning and could remember nothing of the incident. He was duly warned off by the Jockey Club for five years, but by that time he had left the country for a job in Zaire. 'And for all I know, he is still there,' says Peter.

This, in fact, was not the first Derby incident involving paper: in 1882 the clerk of the course was fined £50 by the Jockey Club because paper litter blew into the face of the favourite, Bruce, causing him to shy and lose ground! And in 1831 the winner had to contribute £100 towards policing the course.

From Parachutes to Jumbo Jets

Racehorse transport through the ages

The jumbo jet taxies to the bay at Heathrow where its next load of Australia-bound passengers are waiting. Enough food and drink for the thirty-hour journey is carried on board so that no more will be necessary at the two refuelling stops, both in the Western hemisphere (the Eastern route is banned for fear of picking up disease). Some of the passengers are a little restless but they are soon soothed. Now the time for embarkation has come, and 140 horses, three per pallet, are hoisted aboard.

Over in Kentucky, forty-five yearlings prepare for their trip in a DC8 to bring them to England

Well padded and prepared, an English horse bound for the Arlington Million (USA) boards a British Caledonian 707 at Gatwick Airport.

Horses being loaded at Folkestone Harbour prior to crossing the Channel by ferry.

and the start of their new careers. Meanwhile at Cambridge two of the most valuable horses in the country – no, in the world – prepare for their trip to France, for the Prix de l'Arc de Triomphe. Derby-winner Kahyasi and the five-year-old Mtoto, 'the most improved horse in training', have to have so many staff and security guards between them that there is no room left for any other horses. Even Kahyasi's pacemaker has to travel separately.

Kahyasi has two lads, two security men and a blacksmith travelling with him; a further four men go with Mtoto and there is the flying groom from the company arranging the trip, Horse UK, plus all the paraphernalia they need. When they arrive in Paris they will be met by more security men.

What a far cry it all is from the cloak and dagger stuff that day in 1836. It was known that Lord Lichfield's horse Elis had not yet left Goodwood in Sussex for Doncaster, 200 miles away, so he couldn't possibly walk there and still arrive a fresh horse in time for the St Leger four days later. The odds duly lengthened and Lord George Bentinck, one of the three original 'autocrats' of the turf who masterminded the plan, piled on £1000 at a handsome 12–1. For what he had done was commission the building of a padded, wooden horse-box on wheels, into which Elis was loaded, and he was drawn to Doncaster by a team of six carriage horses who were replaced by fresh ones daily. The result was that Elis arrived a fresh horse and duly won the St Leger, a just reward for Bentinck's initiative and enterprise.

Horses must have been travelling abroad for as long as men have domesticated them; William the Conqueror had to bring his horses across the Channel for the Battle of Hastings, after all. Certainly, racehorses have been travelling abroad to race in France and Belgium since the end of the nineteenth century, usually travelling between

Mtoto and Kahyasi had a plane to themselves to travel to Longchamps for the 1988 Prix de l'Arc de Triomphe. Mtoto was just beaten in the race by Tony Bin.

Folkestone and Boulogne in special freight vessels. They were lifted on in crates, put in stalls and lifted out the other end. When they went to Australia that way, it meant they had no exercise whatsoever for the six weeks of the journey. A member of the crew, or a groom supplied by the shipper, fed them, gave them their hay and mucked out their stalls. The Dutch horses who travelled to the 1932 Los Angeles Olympics were provided with a treadmill on their boat to keep them exercised on the month-long journey.

It was not until 1974 that Australia relaxed its strict regulations on the import of animals and allowed them to arrive by air, but still they are not allowed to stop en route in Africa, Asia or the Middle East, for fear of contracting African Horse Sickness.

On land, the first major advance after the horse-drawn horseboxes was the coming of the railways from 1825. They transformed racehorse transport (and for hunters, mares going to stud and show-jumpers too), carrying them to their destinations in padded compartments with all the speed and smoothness enjoyed by human passengers. Long after the advent of motorized horsebox traffic, much livestock was carried by rail; I well remember my mother's first ever point-to-pointer arriving at Tunbridge Wells West station. He had been

despatched from Ireland wearing tight racing bandages, instead of looser woollen travelling ones, had been 'lost' on a siding for four days and never fully recovered.

Bruce Daglish is the retired managing director of Lep Bloodstock Ltd (now Horse UK), which was founded in the last century as Peden and Son Ltd. The family firm operated from Folkestone and kept sixty transit boxes there until the 1960s, although it had been taken over by Lep Transport after the Second World War. Bruce Daglish remembers horses mingling with passengers on platform 1 at Euston Station on their way to Ireland. This, in fact, continued until as recently as 1970, although the horses were better segregated from humans by then.

Huge, ultra-smooth horseboxes, taking up to nine horses and costing considerably more than some houses, have taken over from rail transport on land, while roll-on roll-off ferries have vastly improved conditions for crossing the Channel – no longer the cumbersome paddlesteamer.

The jet engine has seen air transport improve by leaps and bounds too; horses no longer have to suffer noisy, bumpy propeller-driven aircraft to cross the Atlantic, although such aircraft are still used to fly horses to European destinations, and the old Bristol Freighters, which began horse air

Modern motorized horse transport offers every comfort to its equine passengers.

Train travel was the norm before the deluxe horseboxes of today took over.

It is not only racehorses that travel by air. This picture shows a member of the Indian polo team at Stansted Airport in 1950.

Early air transport was propeller driven. Here a French horse arrives at Blackbushe airfield in 1950.

From horsebox to pallet to aircraft. Transport around the world is made easy for racehorses, whose feed and hay frequently travel with them.

transport in the early 1950s, went out of service only in 1987. Accidents are few and far between and deaths extremely rare, although a BKS Elizabethan crashed at Heathrow in the 1960s; two survivors still live in Newmarket. Horses travelling this way have no reason to think they are not in an ordinary horsebox and there is always expert help on hand in case of emergency.

The flying grooms are knowledgeable, sensible horsemen of high calibre who can sense when a horse is about to have a fit or go berserk; they carry tranquillizers with them and should a year-ling try to climb frontwards out of its stall, for instance, the groom attaches a 'cow collar' round his neck to prevent him. There is at least one groom for every three horses, and in the case of racehorses travelling to a meeting, their own groom goes with them, plus the carrier's travelling groom.

Sophistication, safety, smoothness and speed are the order of the day now, and thankfully no racehorses are on record as having to be parachuted out of aircraft, as was the case with horses in Burma during the last war.

'The Man's a Genius'

Vincent O'Brien

Few, if any, people in the history of horseracing can boast a training record equal, let alone superior, to that of Vincent O'Brien. Those who might aspire to match it under one code, cannot under another, for the remarkable thing about this quiet, soft-spoken Irish genius is that although he has reigned at the top of the flat tree for three decades, his feats under National Hunt rules before that in less than ten years were phenomenal.

Not only has he left his mark on the training of racehorses, he has had tremendous influence on the way horseracing has gone, modernizing the whole business to a degree that few would have envisaged, least of all the young Vincent, who enjoyed hunting and point-to-pointing in County Cork, not a stone's throw from where the first steeplechase was run, in 1752, and landed his first coup in an amateur riders' flat race.

His training career had the humblest of starts, beginning with a 130-guinea purchase from Newmarket war-time sales and a couple of patient owners. By the end of his first season he had achieved a notable success in the Irish Cambridgeshire and Cesarewitch, laying the foundation stone of his future fortune. In 1988, two yearlings from his stud sold for over a million guineas each at the Tattersall's Newmarket Highflyer Sales.

From the start, Vincent O'Brien always planned ahead, paid meticulous attention to detail and displayed admirable patience. He could perhaps be described as a workaholic, never relaxing, never celebrating one big win before making plans for the next one and, ever the perfectionist, always striving to do better – and in particular to make life ever better for the horses themselves. They come first, and that is something new owners quickly have to learn, especially those who think their own diary is more important. This genuine love of horses, whatever their capability,

Vincent O'Brien

is perhaps the biggest secret of Vincent O'Brien's success.

And what success! Between 1948 and 1955, he trained winners of the Cheltenham Gold Cup four times, the Grand National and Champion Hurdle three times each and the Irish Grand National once. What trainer would not be happy to have been connected with just one of his top flat horses, let alone dozens? The names themselves conjure up so much of the history of horseracing since the war: Chamier, Ballymoss, Gladness, Even Money, Larkspur, Sir Ivor, Triple Crown winner Nijinsky, El Gran Señor, Roberto, Thatch, The Minstrel, dual Prix de L'Arc de Triomphe winner Alleged, Try My Best, King's Lake, Golden Fleece and Sadler's Wells, to name just a few.

Although his early years are most associated with National Hunt, even then he ran, and punted, in flat races to a notable degree, and Cottage Rake, the horse who really put him on the map, owed much of his chasing success to the speed he could pull out at the end of a three-mile chase, speed which enabled him also to win a Naas November Handicap and an Irish Cesarewitch.

Turned out on an Irish bog until he was six years old, the small but good-looking son of Cottage twice failed the vet when his breeder put him with the unknown O'Brien at Churchtown in County Cork and tried to sell him. He was nine years old when he won the first of this three Cheltenham Gold Cups in 1948, always ridden by that great Irish horseman Aubrey Brabazon, who went on to train at the Curragh. In his first two Gold Cups, Cottage Rake's speed and Brabazon's skill won the day up the final hill, but in the third, he won virtually as he liked, although it was to prove his last win before a long and honourable retirement back in County Cork.

In 1949, the year of Cottage Rake's second Gold Cup, Vincent O'Brien produced another nine-year-old on the Cheltenham Festival scene, but as this was a hurdler, he could have been considered rather old. Nevertheless, Hatton's Grace also won a hat trick of Champion Hurdles, his last at the age of eleven, as well as an Irish Cesarewitch. By now, all English racing, as well as Irish, was sitting up and taking notice of M. V. O'Brien, who moved in the early 1950s from the wilder landscape of his youth to the lush grass, horse-rearing centre of Ballydoyle, near Cashel, in County Tipperary, just forty miles away.

Hatton's Grace was a small, undistinguished-looking horse who saved his best for the time that mattered, on the racecourse. It is true to say Vincent O'Brien literally transformed him.

Only two years after his last champion win, and three after Cottage Rake's final Gold Cup, Vincent won the Gold Cup again, this time with Knock Hard, another former flat racer who put his speed to good use in the jumping game.

One more jumping ambition burned within him: O'Brien wanted to win the Grand National. Royal Tan had twice somewhat unluckily failed through last fence blunders, but in 1953 Early Mist, bought by the same owner 'Mincemeat Joe' Griffin, put matters right, and the following year

things at last came right for Royal Tan, both horses ridden by one of the greatest National Hunt jockeys, Bryan Marshall, who lives at Compton, Berkshire. His advice to aspiring National jockeys was, 'Let down your jerks, go round the inside and take your time.' Irish-born Marshall predicted Devon Loch as a future National horse when he was retained by Peter Cazalet; in later life he trained and now runs a racehorse-transport business.

As if to set the seal on his career as a mixed trainer, Vincent O'Brien trained the Grand National winner for a unique third consecutive year when Quare Times won in 1955, ridden by that great horseman for ever associated with Arkle, Pat Taaffe.

It was just before his remarkable National era, following close on the heels of his Cheltenham Festival domination, that Vincent O'Brien married

Vincent O'Brien with Ballymoss in the winner's enclosure after the Prix de l'Arc de Triomphe in 1958.

Vincent O'Brien at work at his Ballydoyle stables.
The welfare and training of his horses is always his
first priority.

an Australian woman whom he had met quite by chance; it was a real love match, and the value of Jacqueline's support over the years has been inestimable, a true partnership in every sense.

Before the 1960s began O'Brien had transferred entirely to the flat and set about building a racing empire on a vastly different scale from the typical Irish situation – a farmer rearing the odd horse with his bullocks.

By this time he had been leading trainer in England twice, as well as several times in Ireland. Apart from the principal big races, he had also won no fewer than eleven divisions of the Gloucestershire Hurdle at the Festival. And in 1953, as if to point to things to come, he won not only the Gold Cup and National, but his first classic too, when Chamier won the Irish Derby.

His first really great classic horse was Ballymoss, and his favourite, at least early on, was the filly Gladness. He has superb gallops at Ballydoyle and a purpose-built complex of stabling. No expense is spared when it comes to the welfare, feeding and training of the horses in his care.

It was the chance remark of an owner, Jack Mulcahy, in 1971, by which time Larkspur, Sir Ivor and Nijinsky had each won the Derby, that altered Vincent O'Brien's life. It was simply, 'I can't understand you remaining only a trainer!' It sowed the seed that grew into partnerships, syndicates, shares in racehorses and stallions and the setting up and expansion of Coolmore, now the biggest thoroughbred stud operation in the whole of Europe. To start with, he and Jack Mulcahy bought into the yearling crop of another American friend of Vincent's, Bull Hancock, owner of Claibourne Stud, Kentucky, one of the greatest studs in the world, with marvellous foundation mares and top stallions. From that first partnership crop came Thatch, who became Europe's champion miler. So he was already into the policy of 'having a slice of the action' when he began a similar scheme with Robert Sangster via the super-tough chestnut, The Minstrel, six years later.

Of all the great horses who have been in O'Brien's care, two only two years apart, Sir Ivor and Nijinsky, are most frequently compared in

In 1977 The Minstrel became Vincent O'Brien's fourth Derby winner.

trying to decide who was best of all. As characters, they could hardly have been more different. Sir Ivor was blessed with a phlegmatic temperament and tough constitution, and with a thrilling turn of foot that made him easy to train; Nijinsky was highly-strung and active. Neither Vincent nor Lester Piggott likes to say who was the greater. Both could have won top sprints.

OPPOSITE
Top *Ballydoyle, transformed from quiet Irish farm to leading racehorse training centre by Vincent O'Brien.*

Bottom *Mares and foals at Coolmore, now the biggest thoroughbred stud operation in Europe.*

Sir Ivor withstood a tough campaign and came through with flying colours. Owned by Raymond Guest, the American ambassador to Ireland, who had already owned one Derby winner with Larkspur, Sir Ivor was bred in America and was gawky and overgrown as a youngster. As soon as he won his first race as a two-year-old, Mr Guest placed £500 each way on the Derby at 100–1. A winter spell in Italian sunshine nearly spelt disaster when he decanted his rider on a busy road. Luckily Vincent himself was in the car following behind and leapt out and caught him in the nick of time.

On his way to the Derby, Sir Ivor won in deep mud at Ascot and in the 2000 Guineas, so he started a shade odds-on for the Derby. To his

The easy-going Sir Ivor, ridden by Lester Piggott, wins the 1968 Derby. He went on to win the Champion Stakes and the Washington International.

American breeder, Alice Chandler, and original buyer, Bull Hancock, the race looked lost as Piggott used his supreme waiting tactics, for they were used to the American style of flat-out all the way with digital timing displayed. With only 100 yards to go, Connaught looked unbeatable – then, whoom, out dashed Piggott and Sir Ivor with a devastating turn of speed and it was all over. It was probably the fastest last furlong until Dancing Brave's eighteen years later, but he, poor chap, had been left with an impossible task and failed to add the Derby to his other successes in the 2000 Guineas, King George, Eclipse Stakes and Arc, no less, all in 1986.

In a memorable season, Sir Ivor was beaten by Ribero in the Irish Derby, by the year-older previous Derby winner Royal Palace in the Eclipse and by Vaguely Noble in the Arc; but an easy Champion Stakes win put him back on course for the Washington DC International at Laurel Park in America. Again, the tough colt who seemed to blossom on hard work came up against mud and stiff opposition, but Lester Piggott pulled out another masterly ride and, despite the heavy

ground, Sir Ivor produced his burst of speed for the final time, before returning to the place of his birth to stand at stud.

Nijinsky, by contrast, won the first eleven races of his life, so it was clear from the start that the sky was the limit for him, and it was only in two defeats at the end of his career that seeds of doubt, concerning his temperament rather than his ability, were sown. By the then virtually unknown Northern Dancer, who became the biggest modern influence on thoroughbred breeding, Vincent O'Brien paid top price for him in Canada for new owner, the late Charles Engelhard, in preference to the American's own first choice. So imagine how he felt when, on arrival at Ballydoyle, the colt would not eat an oat, often would not come out of his stable, frequently reared up, sometimes refused to work, often broke out into a lather and generally showed signs of being intractable. But

with skill and patience, not least from O'Brien's staff, who were not exactly enamoured with the bay colt with a heart-shaped star, his energies were channelled in the right direction and he became the first horse since Bahram, thirty-five years earlier, to win the Triple Crown.

He was unbeaten in his five two-year-old starts and not surprisingly he started a hot favourite for the 2000 Guineas in 1970. The first time he was odds against in his life was for the Derby, before which, unknown to any but his anxious trainer and staff, who had already taken every possible precaution against doping, Nijinsky briefly suffered a touch of colic. All traces of stomach-ache had thankfully passed next day when, showing brilliant acceleration under Lester Piggott, he swooped to victory in a time only bettered by his Triple Crown predecessor, and that before there was electronic timing.

When he won the Irish Derby before his enthusiastic home crowd at the Curragh, Nijinsky showed signs of boiling over with all the excitement and sweated profusely, as he had done in his early days at home. It was his ninth consecutive victory and not unnaturally he was being hailed the 'Horse of the Century', an accolade that was underlined when he took on older horses for the first time in the prestigious King George VI and Queen Elizabeth Stakes, including two previous Derby winners, Blakeney and Italian Derby winner Hogarth. He cruised in, showing great maturity, and the St Leger was lined up for a bid at the elusive Triple Crown, before attempting the Prix de l'Arc de Triomphe. Between the Derby and the St Leger, Nijinsky suffered a severe bout of ringworm, which badly affected him. He won the St Leger, his eleventh consecutive victory, but it took much more out of him than any previous race had.

To this day there are many people who blame Lester Piggott for his defeat in the Arc, saying he lay too far out of his ground, confident that the great horse could overtake anything, only to fail by inches, by the shortest of short heads, to catch Sassafras. It should have ended his career on an unbeaten high note, but because of the narrow defeat it was decided to run him in the Champion Stakes, to give him an easy win to retire on. It was not to be. Upset by his milling, cheering fans and a throng of press photographers, he reverted to his two-year-old habits of rearing and being thoroughly

The volatile Nijinsky, brilliantly trained by Vincent O'Brien and last holder of the Triple Crown, seen here after winning the King George VI and Queen Elizabeth Stakes of 1970.

distressed and overwrought. The lovely Nijinsky was beaten by all-the-way leader Lorenzaccio. It is not for this defeat that he should be remembered, but for his brilliant career before it and at stud after it, for this was the proof of the pudding: in later years his sons Golden Fleece and Shahrastani also won the Derby and he was leading sire in 1986.

In Roberto, bred and owned by another American, John Galbreath, Vincent O'Brien had a memorable horse who won the 1972 Derby by the shortest of margins over Rheingold after considerable acrimony over jockeys, Lester Piggott replacing Bill Williamson at short notice. But it is for his great win over the previously unbeaten Brigadier Gerard, bred by his owner, John Hislop, when ridden by an unheard of Panamanian jockey

Nijinsky retired to the Claibourne Stud, Kentucky, and became a successful sire.

in the Benson and Hedges Gold Cup at York, that Roberto is best remembered. Roberto had run unplaced in the Irish Derby and Lester Piggott had opted for Rheingold in the Benson and Hedges, when John Galbreath produced a white rabbit from his hat in the form of Braulio Baezo. A jockey with immense experience in America, he transformed Roberto that day at York, taking him by such surprise with his forcing tactics and even the different way he sat in the saddle that he ran like a horse possessed and, to the utter amazement of the stunned crowd, was never headed.

The year 1975 saw the start of the syndicate and of buying in Keeneland, bringing back to the British Isles blood that had long since gone to America. Syndicates were still unusual at the time, but it was the logical way of producing the extra capital required to acquire the best bloodstock that money could buy. It was before the influx of Arabian money and, with The Minstrel and other top winners among the first dozen yearlings bought, the whole concept got off to a flying start. With success came extra money in the coffers, thus enabling the enterprise to snowball.

The Minstrel was a strong chestnut who belied the saying 'Four white socks, don't buy a horse'. Although very closely related to Nijinsky – they were three parts brothers – the only outward similarity was profuse sweating. Otherwise The Minstrel was a much tougher, calmer character than his illustrious forebear, small and compact with abundant stamina. His grandmother, Flaming Page, bore only three foals, but one was Nijinsky and another became the dam of The Minstrel.

The Minstrel was beaten twice in his life, in the 2000 Guineas and Irish 2000, and was not favourite when he set off for the Derby. Afraid that the noise and general excitement would upset The Minstrel, Vincent O'Brien stuffed the horse's ears with cotton wool; this was taken out at the start by his assistant trainer, John Gosden, who went on to become a leading trainer in America and returned to England in 1989 to take over Lord Derby's magnificent Stanley House Stables at Newmarket, where Gavin Pritchard-Gordon formerly held the reins. He won the Derby in the manner that became his hallmark: resolutely, through guts and hard work. It was the same again when he won the King George by inches, after which it was felt he had done enough to deserve retirement, and he returned to Maryland to stand at stud in the place of his birth.

The greatest feat of Alleged, who was the same age as The Minstrel and became part of the same ownership syndicate, was to win the Prix de l'Arc de Triomphe twice, the first horse since the mighty Italian-bred Ribot, unbeaten winner of sixteen races, to do so. Alleged was only once

David O'Brien's Secreto beats his father's horse, El Gran Señor, after a desperately close race in the 1984 Derby.

beaten in his three-year career; this was in the only classic he ran in, the St Leger, by the Queen's Oaks winner Dunfermline.

His successor as top colt at Ballydoyle, Golden Fleece, was never beaten in a short career and there are many who speak of him in the same breath as Sir Ivor and Nijinsky, something that can sadly never be proved, as he died prematurely of cancer at stud only eighteen months after winning the Derby. Making the tragedy all the more unfortunate was the fact that he was standing in stud in Ireland instead of having gone back to America.

During the 1982 season when Golden Fleece won the Derby, a horse called Assert, trained by Vincent's son, David, won both the French and Irish Derbies. In 1984 confrontation between father and son could no longer be avoided; and the only time El Gran Señor, trained by Vincent, was beaten was the Derby when, in a thrilling photo finish, he went under to the David O'Brien-trained Secreto. David had certainly shown he was a top trainer in his own right, but in 1988 he retired.

These wonderful horses are only the tip of the iceberg. Vincent O'Brien has trained and won with many more from Ballydoyle.

The First Tuesday in November

The Melbourne Cup, Australia

The plumber's little son looked forward to the first Tuesday each November just as much as the rest of his classmates. It was not that he had any interest in horseracing – even though everybody kept saying he should be a jockey because he was so small – but because it meant a whole day off school. It was Melbourne Cup Day, a national holiday throughout Australia, when Parliament does not meet, schools and factories are closed and those not among the 90,000 plus attending Flemington racetrack in their most fashionable outfits are glued to their television or radio sets to listen to Australia's most prestigious race.

Little then did the town boy from the Melbourne suburbs realize that racing would become his life.

He had never so much as sat on a pony, but he admired the only horses with which he did come into daily contact, those pulling the baker's van and the milk float. When a teacher suggested he go to trainer Claude Goodfellow when he left school, the fourteen-year-old Ron Hutchinson jumped at the chance. He never looked back.

Leading juvenile throughout his apprenticeship, he clicked in the saddle from the word go. As soon as he was in the senior ranks, he regularly featured among the top three senior jockeys in the

Melbourne Cup Day. Australia's answer to Royal Ascot, picnics and all!

Australian Ron Hutchinson unsaddling Intermezzo after winning the 1969 St Leger.

state of Victoria (there is no overall national championship). The Melbourne Cup itself eluded him, but that did not prevent him being 'head-hunted' in 1960 by Paddy Prendergast in Ireland. He travelled to the Curragh for six months with the intention of returning for the Melbourne Cup, but stayed instead for two years, followed by sixteen in England, riding principally for the Duke of Norfolk, until he retired in 1977. By then he had more than 3000 winners under his belt, including three English classics, the 2000 Guineas on Martial, the 1000 on Full Dress and the St Leger on Intermezzo, as well as four Irish classics.

Ron Hutchinson and his delightful wife, Norma, his 'greatest asset', agent, weightwatcher cook and confidante, are now based in Australia. But during the years when their principal home was in England – in an unspoilt rural oasis hidden between Reigate and the M25 – there was only one winter, the severest on record of 1962–63, that they did not return home, usually in time for Western Australia's principal meeting, the Perth Cup on New Year's Day. He would ride there until the start of the English season again in March.

In Australia he saw developments in racing that far exceeded anything in England, mainly due to the extra money available since the banning of off-course bookmakers shortly before betting shops were legalized in England in 1961, but also, Ron believes, because the public comes first.

Food available at even the smallest meetings is comparable to any good restaurant without exorbitant prices and with great variety, such as Mexican and Chinese if it is wanted.

And the punter is given every encouragement from newspapers and TV to help him be a winner, whereas in England it is the bookies who seem to get the better end of the stick.

Racing is a pleasant day out for the public in Australia, they can all be under cover on a wet day or enjoy the air conditioning as it is often 100° outside.

It was in the early 1960s that Starting Price bookmakers were made illegal and Tote betting shops came in, with bookmakers still adding their colour on course. The Government takes its cut from the Tote betting shops and the rest goes to the racing clubs, enabling them to increase prize money and upgrade facilities. I can remember visiting the Western Australia country meeting of

Melbourne Cup Day is a national holiday in Australia and crowds flock to Flemington, today as in the past.

Ascot, near Perth, in 1967 and being most impressed that its grandstand facilities were on a par with those of its illustrious royal namesake in England. And although the major British courses have now caught up, very few of the smaller ones have, even though far more people would go racing if it were made attractive for them.

There is very little jump racing in South Australia and Victoria, and none at all in any other state, New South Wales having given it up because it was unpopular. The horses are not bred for it and the one race on a day's card is usually contested by slow, failed flat racers, going as fast as they can for a hurdle race of one and a half miles. Flemington does have a Grand National Steeplechase and hurdle, and there are a few country point-to-points for the enthusiasts, but that is about all.

An exception was the wonderful chaser, Crisp, who captured English hearts with his record-breaking run against Red Rum in the 1973 Grand National and who started his remarkable career in Bendigo.

With the vastness of a country like Australia, populated in total by only 16 million people, racing and training is inevitably centralized, but again the public is well catered for. One of the main differences is that a young horse will never come to the course entirely green, its ability a total enigma to punters, for there are public trials. These are in effect races, with everything present except bookmakers, including cadet stewards.

Trials are held between ten and fifteen horses, complete with jockeys wearing colours, and although most of the trainers will be local, a private trainer like Colin Hayes, for whom Ron Hutchinson's younger son Peter works at Balaclava, will box his horses the sixty miles to take part. The idea is purely educational on the horses' part, they don't have to be 'trying' and they are unlikely to be hit. The days also include barrier (stalls) trials and horses have to have passed these before they are allowed to compete in a race.

In the state of Victoria the premier track is Flemington, home of the Melbourne Cup, and others within a twenty-five mile radius of each other are Ascot Vale, Sandown Park and Epsom

and, contrasting with the English-sounding names, Mooney Valley, Werribee and Caufield. Racing takes place between them by weekly turns. Additionally, there are over twenty country racing associations at venues such as Geelong, Bendigo and Wogga, all well patronized. Racing in New South Wales, where the principal track near Sydney is Randwick, is even more prolific.

Training in Australia is far more on the clock, as in America, with horses timed over a furlong rather than being pitted against each other, as in England. Three times a week, on Tuesdays, Thursdays and Saturdays, the grass tracks are opened for timed fast work. Nor is it just the

horses who are meticulously trained, so are the jockeys, with schools in various centres which every apprentice must attend. Apart from learning the rudiments of race-riding technique, apprentices are given practice in public speaking, attend veterinary lectures, acquire an all-round knowledge of racing and have it instilled in them how to behave and dress properly.

There is very little jump racing in Australia and generally moderate horses participate, but Crisp, seen here in the Aintree Grand National, was the exception.

A race in progress at the Flemington track, complete with attendant seagulls – they make a most unusual spectacle.

The race tracks themselves are beautifully manicured, as I well remember from my visit to the Melbourne Cup in 1967, when the mini-skirt was the height of fashion, although one could not be quite as daring in Australia as in England! In spite of the sun-baked ground, the course itself was a wonderful strip of green, and the race was won by Red Handed, giving trainer Bart Cummings the third of his five successes in the race. All I remember is discovering, too late, that I could have collected some money for my unplaced horse because it was a stable companion of a placed runner and horses from the same yard were automatically coupled for bets.

The Melbourne Cup was founded in 1861 and was a success from the start; even though it was a handicap, it became, and still is, more important than the state Derbies. Some 4000 people watched Archer win the £710 first running, a feat he repeated the following year, but by 1879, 100,000 racegoers were attending the famous race. The biggest crowd of all was in 1926, Spearfelt's year, when a staggering 118,877 attended, and although the figure usually runs in the 80–90,000 bracket, it topped six figures again in 1980, the year Robert Sangster's Beldale Ball won. From the 1970s, prize money leapt ahead and in 1988 was worth some £328,794. In its time it has boasted such winners as Carbine (1890) and Phar Lap (1930), probably Australia's two greatest horses.

Today the standard of racing reaches ever greater heights, for Australia, with its dozen or more million-dollar races, has not missed the attentions of international owners such as Robert Sangster and the Arabs, who have also started up some studs. Begun in the then unfashionable Queensland, the million-dollar races are for horses

Carbine, winner of the 1890 Melbourne Cup and of many other important Australian races from 1888 to 1890.

The sensational Phar Lap, winner of the Melbourne Cup in 1930 and of a total of thirty-seven races. He travelled to America, won a race in Mexico, but soon afterwards was found dead at his stable in California.

who have been sold at public auction in the state, the only ones eligible for the big purse, a lure that has now caught on worldwide, with races such as Goffs Cartier Million in Ireland.

The 1986 Melbourne Cup was won by a horse of Sheikh Hamdan's, At Talaq, who now stands at the Lindsay Park Stud, which is owned jointly by Colin Hayes and Ron Hutchinson. As far as Ron Hutchinson is concerned, the best horse he ever saw in Australia was Burnborough, who in the late 1940s proved himself a really top-class horse by being able to win over distances of

six furlongs one week and one and a quarter miles in record time the next, often carrying huge weights. Trained in Queensland by Harry Plant and ridden by Athol Mulley, sometimes carrying as much as 10 stone 12 pounds, he was an out-and-out champion.

Top *The close finish of the 1988 Melbourne Cup, with Empire Rose fighting off the challenge of Natski.*

Above *The end of an exciting race and the winning jockey receives the congratulations of the huge crowds packed into Flemington.*

The Legend

Lester Piggott

Racing without Lester Piggott would be like a bonfire without flames or a stately home without a nobleman – it would simply not be the same. The pleasure he gave to millions of people over the years has cost him dear. The pursuit of greatness all too often ends in tears: it did for Fred Archer 100 years ago, and it did for Lester in the 1980s.

There are parallels between these great men: both tall for racing, they denied their bodies the source of the very strength that was needed for their greatness; they went to lengths to waste long after mere ordinary mortals would have conceded victory to the scales; both had reputations, at least initially, for an all-consuming desire to win. Both became millionaires yet had reputations for being careful with money.

While illness brought on by wasting led to Archer's premature death, it was at the hoarding instinct that led to Piggott's fall from grace, with a three-year prison sentence in 1987 for a huge tax fraud. Yet despite his own foolishness, wherever one goes in the racing world there is a general air of sadness and sympathy felt for him. He is still held in enormous respect in Newmarket, where he has a reputation as a fair and likeable employer, while to the millions of ordinary punters to whom he gave immense pleasure over the years, he will always be the greatest.

If ever there was such a thing as a racing certainty in terms of human pedigree, it had to be Lester Piggott. Racing down the years has often featured the same names in successive generations, but Lester's pedigree takes some beating, going back over 200 years and six generations to Hampshire trainer John Day (an associate of the Prince of Wales, the future King George IV, in 1775). His son John Barnham Day was a brilliant trainer and the first Southerner to contend seriously with John Scott, the North's great trainer. In the early days of racing there was a distinct North/

Lester Piggott, wearing his St Leger hat, toasts his twenty-eighth classic win.

South divide, with the preference being for the North. Sharp practice and murky dealings were the order of the day in the sport's Dark Ages of the first half of the nineteenth century, and the Days were evidently no exception, for even against that general background, they were singled out for bad reputations.

Happier times lay ahead, as the Golden Age approached and former top jockey Tom Cannon, who rode his first winner at the tender age of nine, took over the Danebury, Hampshire, stables as well as one of the Day daughters, whom he married. Their son, Mornington Cannon, was

champion jockey on the flat six times and won six classics, and Kempton Cannon won three classics, on St Amant in the 2000 Guineas and Derby of 1904, and on Doricles in the 1901 St Leger.

In the nearer family history, on Lester's paternal side his grandfather, Ernie Piggott, was a great rider to hounds, which endowed him with the seat and instinct for survival to win three Grand Nationals, on Jerry M in 1912 and two on Poethlyn in 1918 and 1919, as well as being champion jockey three times. Even before the First World War, he often travelled to France and Belgium, as well as all over England, to ride, before becoming a trainer at Wantage. His son, Keith, Lester's father, won the Champion Hurdle on a horse trained by his uncle. One of the best National Hunt jockeys immediately after the Second World War, he also won the Grand Sefton and Welsh Grand National before he too became a trainer. It could be said Ayala's win in the 1963 Grand National was his greatest training triumph, but really the presentation of his son Lester to an unsuspecting racing world ranks as that.

The racing pedigree was just as immaculate on Lester's maternal side, where his grandfather was Frederick Rickaby, who won three classics, and whose grandfather of the same name trained the 1855 Derby winner, Wild Dayrell. Fred's son Bill was a fine jockey until a car accident in Hong Kong forced him to retire in 1968. Bill's sister, Iris, rode in the only flat race open to women at that time, the historic four-mile Newmarket Town Plate, and won it twice. She married Keith Piggott and in 1935 they had their only child. They named him Lester Keith.

From his start on a tiny pony called Brandy, Lester was a 'natural'. As a child, he was not unduly tall, gaining his extra height as a teenager after he had started racing; as a boy he had a cherub-like face and superb hands; but he also possessed the ruthlessness of his father and the determination and 'grit' of his mother.

The influence of his father, coupled with his own innate exuberance in his quest to win, landed Lester in hot water with racing's Stewards when still a schoolboy and later. He took the racing world by storm amid such controversy that after a few years he was actually banned from his

Lester Piggott won his first of nine Derbies in 1954 on Never Say Die, at 33–1, when he was eighteen years old.

own father's yard by the Jockey Club and had his licence withdrawn for six months. This most unusual course of action in 1954, six years after Lester had ridden his first winner at the age of twelve, had been champion apprentice three times and had already ridden his first Derby winner, Never Say Die, that year, was taken because of, in the words of the Stewards, 'his dangerous and erratic riding both this season and in previous seasons and . . . in spite of continuous warnings, he continued to show complete disregard for the Rules of Racing, and the safety of other jockeys'.

How sad, over thirty years later, that he still had not learned his lesson and showed similar disregard for the laws of the land when it came to his tax and VAT returns, landing himself in jail for fraud in excess of £3 million.

When he was banned from his father's yard as a teenager, he was taken into the home of first one aunt and then another, and under the wing of Jack Jarvis in his racing yard. He learned to curb his behaviour on the racecourse, at least, though ruthlessness in terms of 'jocking off' other riders to gain fancied mounts himself persisted, while stories of his meanness remain legion.

Throughout his career he had a love/hate relationship with those around him, the public adoring him, while owners and trainers on one hand wanted his services and on the other were fed up and exasperated with his taciturnity and unreliability, for if he accepted a ride and a more attractive one came along, he felt little compunction at breaking his original promise. Never one to use two words when none would do, Lester, partially deaf and with a speech impediment, could appear morose, off-hand and downright objectionable, yet when he smiles the more human side reveals itself, shining through the craggy face, pit-lined from years of self-denial. For what, one asks? For pursuit of wins and money – money that he seldom spent.

From the start, attention, whether sought or not, followed him wherever he went. That first win, on a horse called The Chase at Haydock Park in 1948, was followed by six more the next year, and by fifty-two in 1950, but in that year he received his first suspension. The first of his thirty-two rides in the Derby came the next year when, uncharacteristically, he was left at the start on the temperamental Zucchero, for one of his

fortes was understanding and handling difficult horses. He also suffered the first major injury of his career that year when he broke a leg.

He was beaten by only a neck in the Derby of 1952 and in 1953 he rode the first of twenty hurdle race winners in two seasons, the most notable of which was Prince Charlemagne, when he landed a gamble in the Triumph Hurdle at Hurst Park of 1954, having been unplaced on the horse in the Derby the year before.

Of course, he bounced back from suspension with a vengeance, landing his first century of winners; he also landed the country's leading job when he became stable jockey to Noel Murless, later Sir Noel, whose daughter Julie married another of today's top trainers Henry Cecil. Noel Murless sent out the cream of horses from his showplace, Warren House Stables in Newmarket, including Crepello, Petite Etoile and St Paddy. He was one of the most well-respected men in racing, as was his jockey, Gordon Richards, whose retirement opened the door for Lester.

It was not until 1960, when he was twenty-four years old, that Lester first became champion jockey. It was a memorable year in other ways too, for he married Susan Armstrong, thus keeping racing in the family yet again, for she was the daughter of trainer Sam Armstrong and she too had won the Newmarket Town Plate. For good measure, Lester also won the Derby and the St Leger on St Paddy.

But 1962 saw him back on the mat in front of the Stewards, who this time suspended him for most of June and July.

Champion from 1964 to 1971, 1966 proved his best season ever, though he never did reach 200 winners in a season, something Gordon Richards achieved twelve times, without the advantages of evening meetings and plane flights. Lester rode 191 winners that year, and three times rode five winners in a day, from a total of five times in his life. He also ended his long association with Noel Murless, who had done so much to transform him into a more acceptable man in racing. Again, it would appear greed was the reason. Piggott believed he could have his cake and eat it, both riding as a freelance and continuing to have the pick of Murless's string, for whom none of the remaining top English jockeys was available at such short notice. Not without enterprise himself, Sir Noel imported George Moore from Australia,

and Lester had to watch his rear end as he swept the board with Mr Jim Joel's superb Derby winner, Royal Palace.

But Lester's golden years took hold when he teamed up with owner Robert Sangster and trainer Vincent O'Brien; he remained freelance for seven years until having first an understanding with Vincent O'Brien and then a contract with Robert Sangster, but he was riding winners for them throughout the period, notably Sir Ivor, Derby winner in 1968, and Nijinsky two years later. Petingo, Ribero, Athens Wood and Humble Duty were among the other good horses to come his way.

The year 1968 was a vintage one. He won four classics, three of them in England, bringing the home total to thirteen and taking him virtually halfway to Frank Buckle's record of twenty-seven, which had stood since 1827. Sir Ivor was certainly a great, stout-hearted horse with blistering

Lester Piggott with Nijinsky, hailed by many as the 'Horse of the Century'.

acceleration. Besides the Derby, he won the 2000 Guineas and the Washington DC International. Lester won the Irish Sweeps Derby and the St Leger brilliantly on Ribero and the Cesarewitch on Major Rose in what was one of Ryan Price's greatest training feats. Then along came Nijinsky, the first Triple Crown winner since Bahram in 1935.

Quieter years in terms of winners followed without a championship title from 1972 to 1980, but the lucrative classics kept coming in. These included the 1972 Derby with Roberto and the St Leger on Boucher, the 1975 Oaks on Juliette Marny in a year which also saw him ride eight winners at Royal Ascot; and his seventh Derby win, on Empery in 1976, breaking Jem Robinson's

record, which had stood since 1836. On The Minstrel, a tough, bright chestnut with four white socks, he won the 1977 Derby, as well as the Irish Derby and King George, and on Alleged, the last really great horse he rode for Vincent O'Brien, he won the Prix de l'Arc de Triomphe in both 1977 and 1978. He could afford to be more choosy, but that did not necessarily mean he intended to be so; at the end of 1980 he parted company with the O'Brien/Sangster team, evidently by mutual consent. For once, the boot was rather on the other foot, for by keeping his options open until the last minute with his main horses, O'Brien often made Lester let down connections of his supplementary rides unintentionally.

But when one door closes, another one opens. The year 1981 found Lester back in Warren Place, as stable jockey to his former employer's son-in-law, Henry Cecil. He soon showed his thirst for winners was as unslaked as ever by becoming champion jockey again in both 1981 and 1982, when in his late forties.

It was in 1981 that he had part of his ear torn off in a hideous starting-stall accident, yet, determined as always to overcome adversity, only one

week later he won the 1000 Guineas on Fairy Footsteps. He also won the Irish Derby on the magnificent Shergar, after that horse's Epsom Derby winning rider, Walter Swinburn, had been suspended. Shergar won the Derby by a record ten lengths but sadly did not live to make his name as a stallion, falling victim to an Irish kidnap gang after covering just a few mares; he was never seen again and is presumed killed.

Although in 1982 Lester won the title, he discounted rumours of impending retirement and promptly won the Derby again, his ninth, on Teenoso in 1983, as well as his twenty-eighth classic in 1984, on Commanche Run in the St Leger. That year, with rumours about unofficial, unregistered payments to Lester rife following publication of a letter from Henry Cecil to his owners which put the tax man on to him and ultimately led to Lester's jailing, the pair split up. Henry Cecil engaged Steve Cauthen, the brilliant

In winning the 1983 Derby on Teenoso (dark horse, yellow/brown colours), Lester Piggott successfully quelled rumours of his impending retirement.

131

young 'Kentucky Kid' as stable jockey. Lester
Piggott, once more, was on his own.

He rode in 1985 as a freelance. It was difficult,
but he had come back before and he could do
so again. He proved it by winning yet another
classic, this time the 2000 Guineas on Shadeed.
But by now, he really was planning to retire and
was busy fitting out a grand, modern stable in

*Lester Piggott gave the Queen her first classic victory
when he won the Oaks on her filly Carrozza in
1957.*

Hamilton Road, the 'new' side of Newmarket. At
Nottingham on 29 October, he signed off with
every jockey's dream, a winner on his last ride.

Between his first ride on The Chase at Salisbury in 1948 and his last on Full Choke thirty-seven years later, he had swung his leg across a horse to race nearly 20,000 times, and galloped roughly as many miles on their backs over every racecourse in Britain and many, many more abroad, in France, Ireland, the USA, Hong Kong, Germany, Spain, Italy, Sweden, India, Australia and South Africa. He had ridden over 5000 winners, 4315 of them under Jockey Club Rules; in addition to his record twenty-nine English classics, he won thirty-five classics abroad, including fifteen in Ireland and seven in France. Once, in a race in Milan, he rode a winner whose odds were returned at 10,000–1 *on*.

He has been recorded as saying that Sir Ivor was the best horse he ever rode; probably one who gave him as much pleasure was Carrozza, on whom he won the Oaks when only seventeen. This was the first classic victory for the Queen, who led the filly in herself. Probably far more sensitive than he is generally given credit for, the

Lester Piggott followed his outstanding career as a jockey with thirty winners as a trainer in 1986.

stripping of Lester Piggott's OBE while he was in prison, a routine matter, was the ultimate ignominy for him, and it caused a public outcry on his behalf in the letters columns of the sporting and national press.

When he started training briefly, before the courts intervened, many people wondered if he could possibly be as successful in that sphere – so few ex-champions ever have, bar Harry Wragg. And he would surely miss riding so much. But he had grown up in a training stable, had regularly ridden at some of the world's greatest and best-run establishments, and had invaluable assets in his wife, Susan, and daughters, Maureen and Tracy. The answer came with an emphatic thirty winners in 1986, including one at Royal Ascot. In October 1987 he was 'sent down' for three years.

Susan Piggott

In jovial mood. Lester Piggott, with American jockey Cash Asmussen, celebrates his first Royal Ascot win as a trainer in June 1986.

The Stewards granted a temporary licence to his wife, Susan, who ran the yard with aplomb until tragedy struck in August 1988, when she was thrown from her horse on Newmarket Heath and crushed. She lay gravely ill on a life-support machine with a fractured skull and ten broken ribs in Addenbrooke's Hospital, Cambridge. Lester was allowed to visit her twice from prison.

Meanwhile, another temporary licence was granted, this time to their elder daughter, Maureen. Only nine days after Susan's accident, their younger daughter, Tracy, made her race-riding debut a winning one at Leopardstown. The Piggotts and racing were not finished yet . . .

All the time he was in prison, the loyal people of Newmarket said they just longed for the day when Lester would return and train a classic winner. That seemed an impossible dream, for how could the Stewards of the Jockey Club, so strict on security, possibly grant a licence to a convicted criminal, while depriving 'shady' characters of one? But they were aware of public sentiment and in September 1988, a month before the first possibility of parole, the Jockey Club announced they would not be taking further action, holding the view that he had had his punishment by being imprisoned and prevented from holding his licence during that time. There was evidence, they said, that he may have 'seriously damaged the interests of racing', but they added that his imprisonment was 'for civil offences that did not in themselves transgress the rules of racing', and said they were also taking into account his services to the sport.

His release on 23 October 1988 brought with it a new sense of purpose for Lester Piggott, for apart from his future career, his immediate all-consuming efforts were aimed towards helping his wife recover.

'Himself'

Arkle

One of the eternal fascinations of racing lies in trying to compare great horses of different generations, if only because no argument can be proved, thus letting both sides remain convinced that they know the answer.

Such conjectures are different from the conclusive 'race of the century', which from time to time gets billed within a generation, Mill Reef against Brigadier Gerard, and Voltigeur against The Flying Dutchman, for instance.

No one will dispute that Arkle was the greatest chaser of his day. Only a few will claim that he was not the best of all time. But there *are* those who say Golden Miller was the greatest, and with the two horses foaled thirty years apart, many people were able to see both.

Having witnessed only Arkle, I find it unimaginable that any other horse could *ever* match him; and yet a horse in the same yard at the same time, Flyingbolt, is very much mentioned in the same breath by his late trainer Tom Dreaper's widow, Betty, now Lady Thomson. Tom himself remained loyal for a long time to the great Prince Regent, whom he trained in the restricted war era to win eighteen races, including the Cheltenham Gold Cup of 1946 and the Irish National, and come in third, carrying 12 stone 5 pounds, in the Grand National. Prince Regent's sire, My Prince, also sired those great chasers Reynoldstown (Grand National twice), Royal Mail, Gregalach and Easter Hero (Cheltenham Gold Cup twice). Finally, Arkle held sway in Tom Dreaper's opinion, but it must mean that there was not that much between the horses.

Arkle won the Cheltenham Gold Cup three times before a broken pedal bone ended his career prematurely; Golden Miller won five Gold Cups *and* a Grand National (in which Arkle was never risked); Red Rum won three Grand Nationals; Manifesto won two and was placed in it three times; Sir Ken and Hatton's Grace each won three Champion Hurdles; the gutsy Monksfield, Night Nurse and Sea Pigeon each won two. But it is not the *number* of wins but *how* they win that counts, or top-class stallions would be kept much busier on the turf for a start.

Red Rum had to overcome all sorts of different hardships, from lameness to punitive races under assorted jockeys and owners. Golden Miller had an eccentric owner who passed him from trainer to trainer. But Arkle, like Dawn Run in later years, had one devoted owner and one most skilful trainer, a priceless asset. The first two used their spirit to overcome adversity and succeed; the latter two had the great advantage of being able to put all their spirit and character into racecourse performances.

Arkle was a star and to watch him perform was a lifelong privilege. He adored people, and people adored him, so much so that he even joined in games of ball with the Dreaper's young daughter, Valerie. Wherever he went, there was an aura of regality about him, head held high, ears pricked, whole bearing proud. In a race he was poetry in motion, he jumped superbly, he galloped effortlessly.

Once only he was beaten by making a jumping mistake – by Mill House in his first Hennessy; just twice he was beaten by crippling weight; and once he was beaten by injury. He never fell racing and when he blundered wholesale as his attention was diverted by his cheering public, in his third Gold Cup, he learned his lesson, unlike poor Dawn Run. She, hyped up from the tumult after winning at Cheltenham, was nearly mad with excitement and fell at the first next time out and a few races later was killed.

Arkle was bred at the County Dublin home of Mrs Mary Baker, and as a gawky three-year-old was sent to Goffs Sales at Ballsbridge, home of the

Royal Dublin Show. Anne, Duchess of Westminster, bought him, named him after a Scottish mountain and in due course sent him with another of hers, Ben Stack, to Tom Dreaper's yard at Kilsallaghan, as his mother and grandmother had been sent before him.

Not much notice was taken of the unexceptional youngster, for not much was expected of him. His granddam, Greenogue Princess, had won point-to-points ridden by Tom, and his dam, Bright Cherry, could just about last home in a two-mile chase if the going was like concrete. Tom Dreaper, therefore, did not envisage him developing into a three-mile chaser at all, let alone a crack one.

He was unable to win a 'bumper', the two-mile educational National Hunt flat races, to score in which has become the means to 'blank cheque' sales, and when he was despatched to his first hurdle race at Navan, it was very much as the stable's second string. Lady Thomson takes up the story: 'It was over three miles in the mud, and we did not then know whether he would get that distance; also we had a horse called Kerforo in the race, who was the favourite.'

Jockey Liam McLoughlin was accordingly told to let Arkle see his hurdles in the twenty-seven-runner novice race. 'From the stands we could see one horse on the wide outside passing everything else,' says Betty. 'It was Arkle and he won as he liked. Tom said, "I think we have got something there."'

Arkle, indisputably the greatest chaser of his day and winner of a record £57,000 in three years, seen here cantering through the Irish countryside.

The mare Kerforo won three races later that season, including the Irish Grand National. The Navan result had been totally unexpected, but Arkle soon showed it was no fluke. He was also that paragon, a perfect horse to train, easy to care for in his box and to ride, a good 'grubber' and he had a temperament to match. He ran in five more hurdles, won three of them, and later in his life won a maiden plate on the flat as a pre-season warm-up.

For his first ever chase he was taken to England, to Cheltenham no less, for the Honeybourne Chase in November, and after winning that, and a chase at Leopardstown, he returned to Cheltenham for the National Hunt Festival. But although he won the Broadway Chase (now the Sun Alliance), he was not the talking horse of the meeting. That distinction went to a gentle giant of a horse trained by Fulke Walwyn called Mill House, who at only six years old, the same age as Arkle, won the Cheltenham Gold Cup. He was hailed as the new Golden Miller, and it was considered he would scale at least similar if not greater heights.

When Mill House and Arkle first met, amid great press build-up and speculation, it looked as if the English pundits were right. Arkle, who had

won four more chases since the Broadway, slipped at the final open ditch and could finish only third to the mighty Mill House. He was a nice horse, but Mill House had jumped better, given weight away and deserved to win. Naturally, when a renewed clash was lined up for the next Cheltenham Gold Cup, the English would not hear of defeat for their reigning champion, even though Arkle had won his last three chases in Ireland.

Ten minutes before the Gold Cup, as the horses paraded, it started snowing on the heavy ground and it was debated whether to let the horses race. But down at the start the snow stopped (unlike in 1987, when the horses had to canter back to the paddock, eventually to race one and a half hours later). Mill House and his competent rider, Willie Robinson, set off, leading the four runners and jumping superbly. It looked a formality. But not to those watching the Irish horse poised just behind with his regular jockey, Pat Taaffe, himself a fine horseman, and an integral part of the long-standing success story at Kilsallaghan.

When Willie Robinson went for his whip between the last two fences, the writing was on the wall. Pat Taaffe had only to shake the reins at Arkle to take command and storm away up the hill for a five-length win. Pas Seul, himself a previous Gold Cup winner, could only struggle in twenty-five lengths behind, such was the supremacy of the leading pair.

In the future, supremacy belonged to one, although Mill House did again attempt to take on Arkle, and possibly broke his heart in the process. But Arkle won again on their next meeting, in the Hennessy, this time making the running himself. They met again in the Gold Cup of 1965, and set off together, but all Mill House's efforts were futile; he struggled to keep in touch, but when Pat Taaffe pressed the button, Arkle simply drew away to win by twenty lengths.

By this time, many of his races in Ireland were becoming mere 'exercise canters', and the handicappers had a real headache on their hands, for Arkle was so far superior to everything else that all his rivals would be lumped together on bottom weight, two or two and a half stone beneath Arkle. Then, if he did not run, there was no handicap at all. A new system had to be devised, and because of Arkle two handicaps were to be drawn up in future: one for if the top weight runs, the other coming into force, with weights increased in proportion, should the top weight withdraw at the overnight stage.

An Arkle fan club had started, the result, Lady Thomson believes, of television's enabling the public to get to know a horse personally. After his first Gold Cup win, the tiny road leading to his stables was blocked with cars full of admirers. All through the summer tourists from countries all round the world, including Japan, would come knocking at the door, and they were always shown 'Himself', as Arkle became universally known. There would be grannies with prams, children thinking it was fun to slide down the bales in the hay barn and father smoking a cigarette – it became a security nightmare. Even the local council was finally persuaded to put Greenogue on the map officially with a signpost for the first time.

The fan mail also began to arrive in droves – one was addressed simply Arkle, Ireland – and all sorts of things would be sent through the post, like sugar lumps from a pensioner or a can of Arkle's favourite – Guinness. 'It was at about the time of the start of the Troubles, and I can remember taking a parcel into the garden to open, thinking it would be only me hurt if it was a bomb,' Betty recalls. 'It was a carrot.'

At this time the Dreapers had no secretary, all administration being handled by Tom and Betty. In Arkle's last season Betty also had to take over the training when Tom was ill. Then the Duchess of Westminster lent her a secretary, Mrs Tinsley, for one day a week, and Mrs Tinsley is still working for the Dreapers' son Jim, who has become a successful trainer in Ireland himself.

When Arkle went to the post for his third Gold Cup, he started at 10–1 on. Realistically, only a fall could make him fail, and he had never fallen on the racecourse. How nearly he did that day! Cruising into the last fence first time round, at more or less the halfway point in the race and closest to the crowds, a good few of whom were craning by the fence itself, Arkle simply looked at them and listened to the cheers instead of taking off. His chest took the full force of the birch fence and carved a path through it; he and Pat Taaffe between them subconsciously took every action possible to avoid a fall and miraculously they achieved what for a few breathtaking moments looked impossible. It was one hell of a mistake, but Arkle recovered himself and Pat Taaffe,

A rare mistake by Arkle during the 1966 Cheltenham Gold Cup. He went on to win the race for the third year running.

adopting a good old hunting seat, shooting his legs forward and slipping the reins, remained in the saddle.

When he sauntered home by a record-breaking thirty lengths, it was still the mistake everyone was talking about. The sky looked the limit. Only his own stable companion, Flyingbolt, who won the Irish National a month later, Tom Dreaper's tenth in all, could come anywhere near him. Here the fates that put the two horses in the same stable, although Flyingbolt was born in Newmarket, ensured that they would never be asked to take issue together, because Tom was certain one of them would never be any good again.

The handicapper twice got the better of Arkle in his career, in heartbreaking attempts at defying huge burdens, and both times he was beaten by a grey. The first was in 1964. He started the new season after his first Gold Cup win by beating Mill House in the Hennessy (as he did yet again at Sandown a year and a half after that, by then giving the big horse 16 pounds). Arkle pulled Pat Taaffe's arms out, running and jumping like a stag round Newbury, treating any mistakes he did make as if they had not happened. But only seven days later, having not returned to Ireland and running over the shorter distance of two miles five furlongs in the Massey Ferguson at Cheltenham with a 3-pound penalty bringing his weight up to 12 stone 10 pounds, he was unable to give all a second time so quickly. The mare Flying Wild,

carrying 10 stone 6 pounds, and Buona Notte on 10 stone 12 pounds, passed him at the last. He fought back, but was beaten by a head and one length.

It was two whole years before he was beaten again, this time attempting to give Stalbridge Colonist *35 pounds* in the Hennessy. No defeat could have been more honourable, and not all eyes were dry at the sight of it.

Sadly, only two races later, there were to be a good many more tears. Arkle won the intervening SGB chase at Ascot, and his second King George VI chase at Kempton in front of the big Christmas crowd on Boxing Day looked a formality. It was not to be. Somewhere out there as he sailed along, probably at an open ditch, he knocked his off-fore foot so hard on a take-off board or guard rail that his pedal bone was broken. In the heat of the moment, with the adrenalin flowing, neither horse nor rider knew it. Nor did his ardent supporters from the stands, who stared in disbelief as Dormant overtook him on the run-in and beat him by a length. Good, honest horse that Dormant was, he was not a patch on Arkle. Moments later, as he pulled up, it was obvious to all that Arkle was lame.

Betty Thomson recalls, 'At first we were just

The unveiling of the Arkle statue at Cheltenham. Tom Dreaper, Arkle's trainer, is on the left, with the Duchess of Westminster on the right.

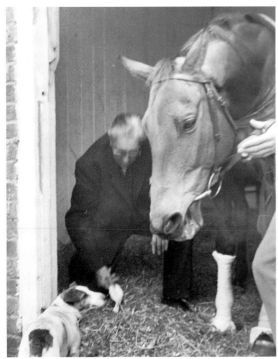

Arkle at Kempton Park Stables, with his leg in plaster after breaking his pedal bone.

amazed that he was beaten because he was in a different class to everything else, then we saw he was lame, and after that there was not much time to think of anything, there was so much to cope with in looking after him.' Arkle stayed in his box at Kempton for six weeks with his leg in plaster, his door and walls smothered in Get Well cards – Jim Dreaper still has boxes of them at his home – and was attended by his own vet, who flew over from Ireland, and also a specialist from Cambridge.

It was hoped that Arkle would be able to make a comeback, but arthritis set in and the dream was extinguished. Four years later, at thirteen and in pain, he was put down and buried at the Duchess's farm in Maynooth, where Arkle had spent his summer holidays and later his retirement. When she sold the farm a few years later, she donated his skeleton to the Irish National Stud at Kildare, where it is on display.

But it is in live action that Arkle is for ever remembered, for his superiority was truly stunning, as his record of twenty-seven wins from thirty-five runs, no falls except once schooling over hurdles and only once unplaced, in a hurdle race, shows.

'We're Amateurs!'

Point-to-pointing

Originally point-to-pointing, run by the local hunt, was just that: hunters raced from one point (or church spire or steeple) to another the best way they could, negotiating whatever banks, brooks, ditches, gates, plough and fences that got in their way. Gradually, as with steeplechasing, courses became regulated, with made-up fences, affording greatly improved visibility for spectators.

There are always those who lament the 'good old days', but generally speaking the sport has only improved. Point-to-pointing remains amateur and there is a great *esprit de corps* about it: the family day out in the country, complete with picnic in the boot and almost certainly a

bottle or two to wash it down with, wellies, rainwear and binoculars. Except in a few cases where old or current racecourse facilities are used, there are no permanent buildings or grandstands; the paddock is a temporarily erected rope ring and flags or dusters adorn car aerials so that the children don't get lost. The bookies do a roaring trade, and although the favourite usually wins (there is no handicapping in point-to-points and only limited penalties), their cramped odds ensure

Bookmakers are part of the point-to-point scene and usually do a brisk trade.

Wellies and warm wear
are the order of the day at
point-to-points.

that they usually go home with their satchels bulging.

To those who moan that the sport has become too 'professional', with one or two big stables mopping up most of the prizes with expensively purchased horses, there are two points: 'professional' means earning a living, which, with token prize money for owners and none for riders, is certainly not the case in point-to-pointing; do not confuse the word with 'proficiency', which should be the goal of any participant wanting to get the most out of a sport. As for the big stables and expensive horses, they are beatable, and that is very rewarding. The slur of being too 'professional'

has in fact been levelled at the sport since as long ago as the 1850s, by novelist Robert Surtees.

On the whole, point-to-pointing still makes an ideal nursery for the young future chaser, and it also makes an appropriate retiring ground for the old one. Of the few top-class chasers who come 'pot-hunting' into the sport while still in their prime, it is up to the hunt committees, who organize the meetings, to include conditions and penalties that will make life distinctly difficult for them, and not all such horses are guaranteed to stay the minimum three-mile distance of a point-to-point.

Hunting is still the *raison d'être* behind point-to-

They're under starter's orders – point-to-points are started by a flag not stalls or gate.

pointing, and all horses have to qualify with a hunt before they can run. Of course, there are those who pay only lip service to this requirement, but this is nothing new. To quote Surtees:

> In the early days of steeplechasing a popular fiction existed that the horses were hunters ... grooms used to grin at Masters requesting them to note they were out, in order to ask for certificates of the horses having been 'regularly hunted', a species of regularity than which nothing could be more irregular.

For many, hunting is all part of the build-up and fun of it; the hunting field is an ideal place for a young horse to learn how to cope with all sorts of unexpected obstacles and terrain, and for the older racehorse sickened of training, it is nine times out of ten a real sweetener. Although virtually all point-to-pointers are Thoroughbreds, the host hunt's members' race is open to non-registered horses, encouraging more 'genuine hunters' to have a go, often for a special heavy-weight prize.

Complaints of one stable winning too many races is nothing new. When Doreen Calder's great-uncle owned and rode all the winners at the East Lothian Yeomanry meeting in 1863, he was asked not to return the next time!

The undulating Border country of Scotland, renowned for its hunting, farming and flower-filled market towns, has been home to many fine National Hunt horses. It is from these parts that Reg Tweedie's gallant Freddie progressed from winning the Buccleuch Hunt members' point-to-point race and seven hunter chases, including the Cheltenham Foxhunters, to winning eight steeple-chases still trained from home under permit. He is especially remembered for battling his heart out twice to be second in the Grand National, in his epic struggle against the American Jay Trump in 1965, when that horse and his amateur partner Tommy Smith gave Fred Winter a dream start to training, and to Anglo the following year.

From here too came a grey, The Callant, bred by his farmer owner, Charlie Scott. He hunted hard and twice won the Cheltenham Foxhunters, together with another eight hunter chases, ridden by Jimmy Scott-Aiton, before joining the local professional yard of Stewart Wight and winning more chases.

Another Buccleuch hunter was Merryman, who on his road to winning the Grand National of 1960

won two ladies' point-to-points for his owner, Miss Winnie Wallace. He also won the Liverpool Foxhunters and Scottish Grand National of 1959, before becoming the first Scottish-bred horse to win the National, in which he was also runner-up to Nicolaus Silver in 1961. More recently

Top *Hunting is an integral part of point-to-pointing. All runners qualify to race 'between the flags' by hunting.*

Above *A rural point-to-point in Ireland, a country which has allowed Sunday racing for a number of years.*

another hunter chaser turned top racehorse, Billy Hamilton's Earl's Brig, who numbered Wayward Lad among his victims, has continued to uphold the sporting honour of the region.

But perhaps the most remarkable of all is a point-to-pointer encapsulating all that is truly amateur about this most traditional of sports. He is a horse who nearly never raced at all due to injury; whose woman rider only began racing at an age when many have already retired; whose owner comes from generations of hunting farmers, his wife going to the races in a wheelchair in her precious last years. He is a horse who has seen controversy – and who has amazingly notched up more than half a century of wins: his name, appropriately, is Flying Ace.

The partnership of Doreen Calder and Flying Ace was the culmination of generations of point-to-pointing in the family. The Calder family have farmed in the Duns area of Berwickshire since the 1830s, with hunters and racehorses always an integral part – at one time the family had the oldest registered racing colours. Doreen's grandfather Frank won some yeomanry races at Dunbar before the First World War and bred a few horses, and her father, Adam, went on record at the time as winning at the longest price ever when the Tote returned 500–1 after his victory on the home-bred Blanerne at Wetherby shortly after the Second World War.

His younger sister, who became Doreen Robson, rode show ponies at Olympia when she was only five years old for Lady Muriel Liddel-Granger, and she also went on to ride point-to-point winners. Adam Calder himself began by riding out for local trainer Stewart Wight, who was responsible for turning out such well-known amateurs as Reg Tweedie, Ken Oliver, Major Ewan Cameron and Danny Moralee. Doreen's mother, Malize, hunted and rode in a few point-to-points, and instructed and worked endlessly for the Berwickshire Hunt branch of the Pony Club.

Their attractive farmhouse, bordered by roses, looks south over their arable land towards the River Tweed and Cheviot Hills; behind climb the Lammermuir Hills, on which the Calders' prize-winning sheep graze, joined in the summer by the horses.

A spectacular departure from the saddle for one contestant in the Pytchley point-to-point.

144

Neck and neck at the last fence in a ladies' open race at Parham.

When Doreen Calder and Flying Ace, to their own surprise, won their first seventeen point-to-points, their achievement was dismissed by Southerners: 'Obviously there's not much to beat in Scotland.' Many of them continued with 'I told you so' when the pair were defeated on their first journey south at the Melton Hunt Club meeting in Leicestershire and then again in most controversial circumstances at the RMC ladies' championship hunter chase final at Chepstow. Not for nothing does Doreen Calder possess true British grit, and the pair returned the next year to vindicate themselves fully. With a new American operation on his throat, a heart that makes 'an amazing noise' and a pedal bone in his foot that was broken in two places, it is a wonder that he ever raced at all.

Doreen herself cannot remember learning to ride, but was always more an all-round horse-woman than an aspiring jockey. The family's groom, Adam Hay, who can remember Doreen being born and who has worked for the Calders since coming out of the army in 1955, recalls her riding a pony called Danae in a basket chair, and whenever possible she spent all her time around the horses. As soon as she was old enough, she hunted with both her parents, and took part in gymkhanas and hunter trials.

A keen member of the Berwickshire branch of the Pony Club, she went on the Pony Club Inter-Pacific Exchange to Australia when she was nineteen, beginning a strong bond with that country. She stayed on for two years, working with Hackney harness horses, showjumpers and mustering cattle ('Their paddocks were eight square miles and when the cattle came at you in the yards, it was quite educational!' she recalls), and has returned twice since. She has also been to South Africa, where she worked as a matron in a boys' prep school.

At this time, the horse at home, a mare called Flying Eye, was being ridden by 'proper jockeys' like Charlie Macmillan and Jean Thompson. Bought privately by Adam Calder from Ken Oliver as a five-year-old by the top National Hunt sire Vulgan, she won thirteen point-to-points and two hunter chases and was placed twenty-five times. Doreen's career actually began on her but she had a fall on the far side of the course at Bogside, from where, having put lead weights in her boots, Doreen had to trudge back!

Doreen then bought a 'vast black horse' called Crichton Castle from a local trainer. Nothing too much was expected of him, so there was little pressure; the combination clicked and Doreen won four point-to-points and was placed in three hunter chases on him.

The first offspring of Flying Eye that the Calders raced was Flying Kit by champion hurdler Saucy Kit. He was highly strung and took a long time to break; he also suffered with a wind problem, but was a very good jumper and won four races before breaking a hind leg at home.

Flying Ace, his full-brother, a strong chestnut with good conformation, was not as difficult, and in later years was remarkably amenable, taking

fuss and bother in his stride. Nevertheless, he also had to be broken slowly; he was shown in hand for education at two years and under saddle at four. Doreen also competed in hunter trials and team chases on him and found he was a natural hunter. Like any horse of hers, he was kept for all-round pleasure riding and not exclusively for racing, and, she says, he could have excelled in any sphere, three-day eventing or even dressage.

At six he was being prepared for point-to-pointing (having been turned down by Michael Dickinson at four because he would need more time) when, on his last day hunting, he smashed his pedal bone. He limped into a trailer on three legs and was in plaster for six weeks. Even when that came off, he was still lame. But time proved a great healer, although he is still shod very carefully. The family trait of wind infirmity was also apparent, but the Edinburgh Royal Dick Veterinary College, only an hour away, operated on that with a new technique, tying his larynx back with a piece of stainless steel wire.

He returned at seven and was working nicely, 'but they're all fast past a gorse bush!' laughs

The aptly named Flying Ace with his rider Doreen Calder and owner Adam Calder after winning the Horse and Hound Cup.

Doreen, and when he first appeared in the Berwickshire hunt members' race, she still did not consider him anything extra special. He won that, by a not over-impressive couple of lengths, and turned out again the next week at Alnwick for the seventeen-runner Percy Hunt restricted open race. He seemed mesmerized by the throng and was left nearly a fence at the start; still 'green' and looking all about him, he jumped the first four fences big and carefully.

Suddenly he got his act together. At the end of the first circuit he was still sixty yards in arrears – but he won the race by two lengths. Not surprisingly, Doreen (to say nothing of the spectators) thought, 'This is it!' From then on, the pair became virtually invincible; they climaxed that first season by winning the Vaux novice hunter chase final at Sedgefield and won on their first nine starts the following year. 'He just kept on lengthening his stride and pulling out that little

bit more,' says Doreen. 'Then things started going wrong.'

Her style of riding was criticized when she was left at the start and beaten at Melton, though no less an expert than Jonjo O'Neill, who saw her riding at the new seaside National Hunt course at Edinburgh in later seasons, noted 'There were no flies on her'. Then came the Chepstow débâcle.

She walked the attractive, undulating track with her father and Charlie Macmillan and formed the opinion that the course was twice round. The three-mile start was not marked, there was no map of the course in the changing-room, and when she reached the start and asked the starter he told her he was a flat-race starter and did not know. (The men's and ladies' hunter chase championships were held as the first two races on an otherwise all flat card on the May Bank Holiday Monday). It was only when Doreen, still lobbing along towards the rear, noticed the leading riders with their whips out that she realized the race was finishing a circuit earlier than she thought. She pulled out all the stops on Ace and made up a tremendous amount of ground over the last three fences, but it was too late and they came a fast finishing fifth.

Naturally she had to face the Stewards; she also had to bear with a highly critical press, forgetful that 'We are all amateurs who have very few rides under Rules' – and try and explain to her friends and fans back home. All she wanted was for the ground to open up and swallow her, furious with herself and sad for Flying Ace and his 'supporters' club'. Doreen did not make excuses for what happened, but told the truth and suffered for it: if she had pretended that she thought the horse had gone lame or been off-colour, who could have refuted it?

If the end of the 1984 season was a time to forget, 1985 was truly a redeemer; Flying Ace was first past the post in all his eleven races, although he was disqualified from one when his weight cloth came off just twenty yards from the post. Nevertheless, it was naturally a very apprehensive Doreen who went to Chepstow again in May, determined to get it right this time. It was pouring with rain, and nerves were not helped when the women riders were kept circling fully twelve minutes at the start while one runner was reshod.

It proved to be one of the great races of the season, and for a long time it looked as if Flying Ace was going to be beaten. He fought hard and long all the way up the Chepstow straight as Carol Lee and Majetta Crescent maintained their lead; Ace did not help his cause by jumping right-handed, a tendency he shows under pressure. The pair were in the air together at the last. Majetta Crescent held a slight advantage on the run-in; it *looked* as if he had held on to the line, and in fact went into the winner's enclosure. After a nail-biting twenty minutes, while the judge studied the photograph minutely, Flying Ace was declared the winner.

And to cap the most memorable week of the Calders' life, five days later they beat the favourite for the Horse and Hound Cup Final champion hunters chase at Stratford in great style, the first Scottish horse and the first woman rider to win this race. As the family groom, Adam Hay, said, 'They deserved it for all the work they put in; Ace is part of the family now, the easiest horse to look after, and I am lucky enough to be paid for it.'

By the spring of 1988, Flying Ace was clearly on target for notching up fifty wins. The pressure of the press and TV build-up on Doreen was enormous. Anything could go wrong; the horse had uncharacteristically been on the floor twice in 1986, and she just wished she could get the race over with. The crowds came pouring into Perth to watch 'their' horse, and he did not fail them. He led from the start, jumping brilliantly to beat twelve others, and won again ten days later at Hexham, which was Doreen's personal fiftieth on him, having missed one through injury.

So Flying Ace had passed the magic fifty. Crudwell won fifty under National Hunt Rules between 1949 and 1960, and Lonesome Boy won sixty-five races 'Between the flags' over both banks and fly fences between 1950 and 1959, fifty-three of them in succession. In October 1988 Flying Ace took part in the twice-daily Personality Parade at the Horse of the Year Show alongside Grand National winners Red Rum and Corbiere, who died shortly afterwards. Then it was back to the hunting field and preparation for the 1989 hunter chasing season for Flying Ace.

Sadly, Doreen's mother was not there to witness the landmark of her daughter and their splendid home-bred horse, having died in 1985, but the quiet smile and proud eyes of Doreen's father said it all for a family which is the epitome of sportsmanship.

Full Circle

Arab racing

The car bumped over the stony track by a minuscule hand-made arrow off the maze of narrow Leicestershire lanes. That was all the signposting there was to the Arab race meeting, and it was soon apparent that the only spectators there were those connected with the handful of runners. Bookmakers were not allowed for another year.

The course, a trainer's gallop, was rough and highly unsuitable for racing pace, and the facilities were nil. At least a point-to-point provides a tent to change in! Officials too were obviously unused to the racing scene, but like everyone else present, the heart was willing and they tried their best.

The owner of the horse I was to ride came bustling up, she and her 'support crew' wearing badges bearing the name of their horse. I hoped their confidence would be justified and that her pride and joy would not break down on the going. One thing Arab horses have is a tough constitution and my mount, at 15.3 hands big for an Arab, made mincemeat of his rivals. While not giving the same 'feel' as a powerful Thoroughbred, it is lovely to ride a winner at any time, and the

Arab racing was introduced in Britain in 1978 and the season culminates with a big international meeting at Kempton Park.

Mrs J. Barlow rode Imman to victory in the 1985 Guinness Stakes at Kempton.

delighted connections embarked on their long journey back to Sussex all of £30 richer. But when you own a racehorse of any calibre, it is not wise to add up the cost of entries, keep, fees, etc. in relation to prize money. By far the vast majority make their owners a loss.

The Arab Horse Society, well known for its show horses and studs, decided to branch into racing in 1978, with the blessing and under the watchful eye of the Jockey Club. After all, it was pure-bred Arabs who were so influential in founding the Thoroughbred racehorse. To begin with, there were just two meetings. The first was at Hawthorn Hill, Berkshire, on 10 July 1978, when thirty-one horses took part and the whole thing was truly amateur. In 1983, seventy-five horses ran, ridden by sixty-one jockeys, and the infant sport was gradually making progress, when in 1984 it received an almighty shot in the arm from the Arabs, already well established with their racehorses in England, who decided to sponsor Arab racing.

Suddenly, its maximum prize money leapt from £65 to a staggering £4000, and the following year, at the inaugural 'show case' international meeting at Kempton, the first prize for the Dubai Stakes was raised to a phenomenal £8500, something that has never happened in point-to-pointing.

Not unnaturally, everyone wanted to jump on the bandwagon, virtually any horse with Arab blood became a potential Arab racehorse (the sport was too young for any specific race breeding to have yet taken effect), and participants quadrupled. But there was a minus side, for the sport nearly fell victim to its own success, for so much balloting out was having to take place that some owners, faced with the cost of keeping and the effort of training, found their horses getting only one or two runs in the season. Happily, in 1988, with the number of meetings increased to fifteen, there was less balloting out than in 1987. The meetings are held from May to October, all on licensed racecourses bar the two at Larkhill point-to-point course in Wiltshire, an army venue which has permanent buildings, and all runners are graded, with races framed to match ability.

Crowds are increasing and the standard of racing is steadily improving, although races for part-bred Arabs have been banned, following a 'ringing' scandal in 1987 which went to court in April 1989 and resulted in a prison sentence for the Kent trainer, Christopher Willett. In 1987, 406

Kim Bradley on Carabineer after winning the £8500 Dubai Stakes at Kempton's international meeting.

horses and 312 jockeys took part, but happily, in spite of the money put in and the huge increase in participants, Arab racing remains amateur, an ideal schooling-ground for the potential jockey and above all an outlet for the genuine amateur to own, train and ride his own horse.

Ex-professionals who have not held a licence in the last five years are also allowed to train or ride. This enables someone like Kevin Gray to participate. A former National Hunt jockey, he suffered one of the greatest fears of a jump jockey's life – a broken back at the age of only twenty-one. It spelt the end of his promising career, and he had to spend a year in hospital. Ten years later, he

OPPOSITE

Aintree 1987. Racing of a different kind takes place on the famous Grand National turf. Kerim Bey (No. 5) and Count Shazariee do battle (top), while the bottom picture shows the field rounding the grandstand turn.

jumped at the chance Arab racing offered and ended the 1987 season as leading jockey with nine winners. Poor Kevin's luck was not to last: in 1988, returning from the gallops, the Thoroughbred he was riding collapsed and died, breaking Kevin's leg in two places and forcing him to miss the whole of the 1988 season.

By contrast, Sue Wilkinson, a secretary from Yorkshire, bought her horse, Ashmahl, for £400 as a two-year-old and in 1987 she owned, trained and rode him herself to win the £8500 Dubai Stakes at the International meeting at Kempton, taking on and beating the challenge from France. Her refreshing success and a similar one by Oxfordshire's Kim Bradley in 1986 were sandwiched between two whitewashes of British horses by the French.

In 1988, when the Emirate of Dubai supported Arab racing to the tune of £85,000 for the fifth year, the French not only won the Dubai Stakes but also filled the first three places in the other international race. The Dubai Stakes lived up to its international status, with a Russian horse second, a British one third and one from Sweden fourth. The sport has certainly progressed from its humble beginnings just over a decade ago.

Sheikh Hamdan Bin Rashid Al Maktoum presents the Dubai Stakes trophy to Kim Bradley.

151

'The Mare'

Dawn Run

The stunned French crowd, already sweltering in the heatwave, stared in disbelief. The English visitors barely held their emotions at bay. The Irish contingent wept openly. 'Their' mare was dead.

Lying out there on the luscious green sward, her neck broken, was the mare who had been ridden to her first victory by her veteran female owner, a grandmother who had stolen Irish hearts long before the horse herself did; the mare who had nearly died as a foal on the County Cork farm where she was bred; the mare who had been champion hurdler of *three* countries, and who had finally broken the hoodoo and become the first horse ever to achieve the Champion Hurdle/Gold Cup double. She was the mare for whom unique was not too strong a word: Dawn Run. Now she lay dead under the blazing Paris sun. The disbelief turned to vitriol. Seldom has such venom been spat at an owner as on Friday, 27 June 1986.

The ripples spread over the Curragh, scene of the next day's Irish Derby, more like a bomb thrown in an ocean than a stone in a pond. 'Greed!' the mob cried, in almost universal condemnation, referring to Mrs Charmian Hill, the diminutive, wiry owner whose own courage had often been hailed as much as that of her mare, a pair of Irish heroines. Everywhere the feeling was that the great Irish mare should have been allowed to rest on her laurels after her unique and utterly memorable victory in the Cheltenham Gold Cup. The accusation that Mrs Hill killed her champion was still rife two years later, and it was also ridiculous.

It could as easily have happened in the first race of the season as the last; she had not run until December, so was not overraced; and she had proved in the past that she was a 'spring' horse, as when she had added the French Champion Hurdle to the English and Irish ones she won in

1984. Even then, connections had been berated for keeping her in training until June, a decision that was fully vindicated by her victory.

Every likelihood was that she would now repeat that triumph. New jockey Michel Chirol, a French champion, pulled her ears as they emerged on to the racecourse before taking the customary practice flight. There, the English runner and Dawn Run's rival of old, Gaye Brief, fell, as he was to later in the race as well.

Thanks to Auteuil's watering system and excellent ground care, the going was perfect. Dawn Run looked a picture and Chirol a faultless partner. He was clearly just biding his time as she went into every flight sharing the lead, and came out of each one two lengths clear – until, that is, the flight on the far side, the fifth from home. Then she never reappeared at all. It is not for her death that Dawn Run should be remembered. Hers was a truly remarkable career, not least because it was so unlikely.

Breeding was a hobby for John Riordan, and when the filly foal ran such a high temperature that recovery looked forlorn, it was only one in a long line of setbacks that beset every small time National Hunt breeder. It was thanks to his wife, Prudence, who spent many sleepless nights willing the foal to feed, that she recovered.

It was as a three-year-old that Charmian Hill bought her at the Ballsbridge Tattersall's Sales for 5800 guineas and, already well into her sixties, had very soon backed her. Although big and green, Dawn Run was so quiet to handle that when Mrs Hill felt she was ready to join her trainer, Paddy Mullins, she warned him, 'I'm afraid she may never make a racehorse, she's so placid.' But it took only one race for Dawn Run, beautifully bred for chasing by Deep Run out of an Arctic Slave mare, to become competitive. That was to become her trademark. She was not

necessarily always the best horse in a race, but she invariably tried hardest, and it was her guts and courage that won her fame.

Charmian Hill herself opened Dawn Run's account, in her third run in a bumpers' in front of a holiday crowd at Tralee, and when, much to her disgust, the Irish authorities refused to renew her licence to ride on the grounds of her age, trainer's son Tony Mullins took over. From then on, until her last fateful race, most of her runs were shared between Tony and Jonjo O'Neill, the genial Irishman who became England's champion jockey, who rode her to both her Champion Hurdle and Gold Cup victories.

Here too there was controversy. When Dawn Run first set out on the path to stardom, her meteoric rise had not been foreseen and Tony Mullins was a young, inexperienced professional. Once the big time beckoned, Mrs Hill felt only the best would do, hence Jonjo was engaged. But when he was injured, the ride reverted to Tony, for whom the mare, in her own utterly feminine way, undoubtedly went well. Mrs Hill felt he still had a lot to learn, though, so she engaged Jonjo whenever possible.

Dawn Run on her way to victory in the 1984 Champion Hurdle, ahead of Buck House with Desert Orchid between them.

Although hurdling was only ever considered a means to an end, a stepping-stone and schooling-ground towards chasing, Dawn Run gave clear notice at the end of her first season that she had a turn of foot too, when running that year's champion hurdler, Gaye Brief, to a length at Liverpool in April. At home Mrs Hill still often rode Dawn Run herself on Paddy Mullins's circular field gallop – and it was hard to say who was enjoying it more.

Gaye Brief was an odds-on ante-post favourite for the Champion, but the press had begun to sit up and take much more notice of the Irish mare. By now, with the Irish Champion Hurdle also under her belt, she had established herself as a bold front runner who liked to do things her own way; if challenged, she did not give in, as others were to find to their cost. She was a great-hearted battler and a relentless galloper who stayed for ever.

In the end, Gaye Brief could not start for the Champion Hurdle, and it was left to Dawn Run to take advantage of the new 5-pound mares' allowance and throw off one challenge after another; nearly all the runners tried at some stage to take over, but none succeeded. She beat the gallant Cima by three-quarters of a length, with Very Promising third and her old Irish sparring partner Buck House fourth.

When it was decided to take Dawn Run to France that June it was to tackle the strange 'hurdles', more like mini chase fences but ones that could be jumped from both ways, which have been the downfall of many an English challenge. One of the respects in which Dawn Run proved so remarkable was her adaptability, and when she treated the French race like any other, it was greeted wholeheartedly by the French spectators and the vociferous Irish band. It might not have provoked the incredible scenes that Cheltenham did, but there was not too much staid decorum about it either.

So Dawn Run returned victorious to the Waterford home of Charmian Hill and her doctor husband, Eddie, to roam at will during the calm summer months. Next season she would go chasing, on that Charmian was quite determined, in spite of increasing pressure to keep the mare hurdling while the pickings were still rich.

It was in November that she made her chasing debut at Navan, and it was unforgettable. She ran in only seven steeplechases in her life and gained a poor jumping reputation, yet on that first day she performed as if to the manner born. Only once was there any semblance of 'meeting one wrong', and even then there was no discernible mistake. She put Dark Ivy and Buck House emphatically in their places; ironically, all three horses were to be dead within three months of each other three years later.

Immediately a 'new Arkle' was hailed, the 'Dawn' of a new era; already odds were quoted for the 1985 Gold Cup. But her fans had to wait another full year for that. A minor setback kept her off the course for thirteen months. She immediately won her first two chases in Ireland on her comeback, and when she was quoted favourite for the Gold Cup, there were those who derided the decision as absurd for such a novice. Fuel was added to the fire when meeting stiffer fences in a prep race at Cheltenham in January she unseated Tony Mullins. Her next race, with only four chases behind her, was the Gold Cup itself – and Jonjo was booked to ride.

Cheltenham in March is invariably as cold as its

In 1986 Dawn Run, seen here jumping beside Run and Skip, became the first and so far only horse to complete the Champion Hurdle/Gold Cup double.

atmosphere is warm. Traditionally there is great friendly rivalry between the English and Irish, both of whom, naturally, display their very best goods in this supreme shop window. The amphitheatre beneath Cleeve Hill makes an ideal setting, and vastly improved stands and facilities make even the biggest crowds bearable. Crowds there were on Thursday, 13 March 1986: a record 41,732 had come to see The Mare and her supporting cast. It proved to be a race that will be remembered for all time in the annals of horseracing.

With Run and Skip in the race, Dawn Run could not have things all her own way, as that gallant little horse set off in the lead, living up to his name. The mare was soon in front, where she liked to be, and had it been any other horses or any other race, one would have thought they must run each other into the ground. She made a slight mistake at the eighteenth, allowing Run and Skip back into the lead, but the mare fought back and hopes remained high as she led over the penultimate. But the pack was closing on her tail.

Suddenly she was no longer all over the winner. For once she had no answer, as first Wayward Lad and then previous winner Forgive 'n' Forget overtook her going into the last. She would, at best, be an honourable but well-beaten third; perhaps too much euphoria had been allowed to surround her.

Jonjo O'Neill salutes the crowd after his famous victory on 'The Mare' Dawn Run.

Charmian Hill leads in Dawn Run with her son Oliver. She always wore her own racing colours.

Dawn Run at the start of her last, fateful race at Auteuil, Paris.

Most eyes were on the two new leaders as they landed over the last fence, with only that uphill slog to the winning-post remaining. But what was this? The Mare was coming again: Dawn Run was storming up the hill; Jonjo O'Neill was galvanizing her. This greatest of all racehorse battlers was refusing to be beaten. The unthinkable a few moments before had happened: Dawn Run had won!

All the pent-up emotion, the slight feeling of anticlimax as she appeared beaten at the last, then the elation of seeing the incredible transformation in those last vital, stirring seconds up the hill – all were now released into scenes of crazy cheering and frantic running as hordes of fans scrambled to reach the winner's enclosure to greet her. Dawn Run – the first horse to win the dual hurdling/chasing crown since the races' inauguration in 1927 and 1924 respectively; a mare, what is more; and in record time too, for she had clipped nearly two seconds off the previous best time.

It was indeed the crowning glory for Dawn Run, and who is to say she would not have won the title again in years to come. She was not another Arkle, that had long since been conceded, but she had her own special brand of enthusiasm and fire, one that endeared her to her scores of followers.

After Cheltenham there was the ultimate anticlimax, for at Liverpool, meeting the first fence perfectly, she simply missed it out altogether and rolled headlong. She was on her feet in a trice, and as she was led back she was furious to be missing the race, running circles round her handler, stamping her foot and tossing her head. Perhaps it would teach her a lesson.

Sadly it did not, although her next outing was memorable. It was a specially arranged match against Buck House in Ireland over only two miles. The shorter distance might have suited the Queen Mother Champion chaser, but Dawn Run showed herself as versatile as ever. Reunited with Tony Mullins, Jonjo O'Neill having now retired, the pair left Buck House standing, even though crack Irish jockey Tommy Carmody more than once tried to steal through on the inside.

And so it was back to France, and this time the heroine did not return. Her death was a grievous loss to racing, to the Mullins family and to Charmian Hill, for whom Dawn Run could have eased her recent widowhood, both by racing and as a brood mare in the paddocks at Waterford.

Recruits for the Big Time

The British School of Racing

Sean Mulvey stood in front of Major Barney Griffiths to explain why he wanted to be a jockey. An Irishman from South Wales, weighing only 7 stone at the age of sixteen and a half, he helped his uncle train greyhounds, he said, getting up at 5 a.m. to exercise them before going to school. He had never ridden, but Major Griffiths, Director of the British School of Racing at Newmarket, surmised he was the right sort of material.

From hundreds of inquiries a year, Sean was accepted for a place on the ten-week intensive course. Like others who had never ridden before, he was started off on a pony in the indoor school, graduating to old racing stalwarts like Path of Peace and Migrator as he progressed. From the start, Sean had lovely hands and sat still with a longish rein. He had style, confidence, that little bit of something. He joined Dick Hern when he left in April 1987, and in June 1988 he had his first ride in public for him.

Hundreds of starry-eyed kids dream of becoming a famous jockey. In reality, only a few get rides at all, and to break into the big time needs

Major Barney Griffiths (second from right), Director of the British School of Racing and its Chief Instructor, with tutors Jane Briscoe, Gary Honeywill, Assistant Senior Instructor Bryan Leyman and Senior Instructor Brian Connorton on the right.

not only skill, dedication, determination and flair, but a good manner and appearance – and, above all, luck.

The Racing School came into being in 1983, after a 'trial run' of eight years at Goodwood. As big yards were getting bigger, time was no longer being spent on apprentices, with the head lad taking the new boy aside and showing him the ropes, instilling discipline and standards.

In the old days, lads 'did their two' and turnout was immaculate. Today, almost invariably, they 'do' three horses and sometimes even four. The pressure is much greater and there is not enough time to spend on the new kid. The days of the Sam Armstrongs and Stan Woottons of this world, brilliant at training apprentices from the 1930s to the 1950s, are gone. Today, fifty or more yards in Great Britain top 100 horses, and people like Henry Cecil and John Dunlop are verging on the 200 mark. A lad (or lass) is apprenticed for only one year nowadays, instead of five or seven years as in the past.

The British School of Racing, run by the Apprentice School Charitable Trust, acquired a 118-acre site down Snailwell Road, past the stables of Geoff Huffer and Pat Haslam, by the lifesize statue of Hyperion at Woodland Stud, past the

The British School of Racing, opened in 1983, is set on the edge of Newmarket.

Equine Veterinary Research Station and the Racecourse Security Services Laboratories.

Purpose-built at a total cost of £1½ million, with the aim of giving it the most modern and comprehensive facilities available, equal to any in other racing countries, it is spaciously set out amid lawns, shrubs and newly planted trees donated by many of Newmarket's leading personalities, each name recorded on a plaque. There are lads' and girls' dormitories, a modern office complex, the traditional stable yard and American 'barn' stables. There is an all-weather gallop which runs parallel to the old airstrip perimeter road, enabling the instructor to drive alongside his protégés, issuing instructions from his window as they go.

OPPOSITE
Top *Apprentices setting off for morning exercise on 'schoolmaster' horses.*

Bottom *Life is made to resemble a training yard as much as possible.*

Major Griffiths uses a Land Rover to keep up with his pupils and issue instructions during exercise.

Of necessity a strict disciplinarian, Major Griffiths runs the school along the lines of a boarding school. A career officer in the Royal Welsh Fusiliers until he resigned his commission to undertake the school's directorship, he was a successful amateur and rode out for many different stables. His background means he has not only the qualifications for assessing basic stable management and raceriding potential but also the ability to instil the importance of manners and smartness in his recruits, who come from many different walks of life.

There was one lad from Liverpool who had never so much as stroked a dog or a cat in his life, but he was a trier and had the necessary enthusiasm. By contrast, some of the girls, who almost invariably have riding experience, are far more likely to resent being told what to do. Boys who can ride are like gold-dust, Major Griffiths says.

Five courses are held each year, with about twenty pupils on each. Aged sixteen or seventeen, boys can be up to seven stone and girls up to eight

(to allow boys greater room for growth). On average, three of those twenty will be aiming at National Hunt yards, and usually there will be twelve boys to eight girls. A high standard is aimed for, and of the 85 per cent who pass at the end, all go into racing but only about 15 per cent will get rides. They are taught how to change hands and use the whip, often sitting on straw bales to practise. The setting is as like a racing yard as possible; they get up at 7 a.m. and 'first lot' is in the indoor school at 7.30. They spend two or three weeks there and the next three sorting things out for themselves; weeks seven to nine are for riding different horses and generally polishing themselves up. After four weeks, they have to pass an assessment.

Every afternoon there are lectures, videos, films or TV racing to watch and the bales work. When one lot is out riding in the morning, the others

will be learning stable management, mucking out, tack cleaning, grooming ('strapping' in racing parlance) and so on. During their course, they will go on at least three visits: to racing either at Newmarket or Huntingdon, according to the time of year, to the National Stud, to the Horseracing Museum, to the Equine pool and so on. They hold a sports afternoon and at the end of the course there is a quiz. For evening stables each pupil has only one horse in his care and he is expected to turn it out to the highest standard, including such detail as washing out the manger, and he will lay out his grooming kit and stand at his horse's head, awaiting the trainer's evening inspection.

Major Griffiths, who also acts as Chief Instructor, is assisted by Brian Connorton as Senior Instructor, Bryan Leyman as Assistant Senior Instructor and two other instructors.

Increasingly, trainers are sending their own young staff on the courses, which now accounts for about half the intake, and the remainder are selected by letter and interview by Major Griffiths, who has the task of whittling down some 250 applicants for about fifty places in a year.

To begin with, forty-five trainers, or one-tenth of the country's total, took advantage of the school, but after twenty-five courses this number had trebled. Regular early supporters of it were Luca Cumani, Susan Piggott, Gavin Pritchard-Gordon and Sir Mark Prestcott. In 1984, just one ex-pupil had a ride in public, and this was Alison Harper, who was apprenticed to Jeremy Hindley. The number increased to fifteen in 1985, doubled to thirty the following year, and in 1987 fifty-three ex-pupils rode on the flat (as well as some over hurdles) and eleven of them rode thirty winners.

It is hard for any kid to break into the big time, but on the whole, it is harder for girls. 'Generally speaking, they don't have that extra bit of strength in the last vital fifty yards and it is harder for them to get the opportunities,' said Major Griffiths. 'They have really got to want to do it.'

Girls and lads learn stable routine, which is as important as learning to ride.

Running Commentary

Peter Bromley

Until Goodwood pioneered a race commentary in the early 1950s, all races were run in complete silence. The idea of a commentator, moreover, met with strong Jockey Club disapproval: it could influence the judge, it could highlight malpractices publicly; and anyway, racegoers read their own races, didn't they?

Surprisingly, it was still a time when knowing the number of runners for a race in advance was a very hit-and-miss affair: twelve runners could appear in the morning paper, as the result of a diligent reporter's efforts to try to establish some facts, but on the day six could go to post. 'The public came a poor fifth in those days,' says one of the earliest commentators, Peter Bromley. There were no four-day or overnight declarations; original entries and trainers' announced plans were all they had to go on. In November 1988, the system was changed again with the introduction of entries only five days before a race (instead of three weeks for most ordinary races), followed by overnight declaration/withdrawal.

With poor prize money in the 1950s, betting was the only way many small stables could survive, but it was very much a closed shop. An ordinary member of the public, who had to go to the races in order to see what was running, stood little chance of achieving a coup, even though he

Glorious Goodwood, pictured a century ago, which in the early 1950s became the first racecourse to give a running commentary.

Peter Bromley, for thirty years the BBC's radio racing commentator.

went armed with his much studied form books and his binoculars.

Obstructed visibility is a commentator's nightmare, but Peter Bromley feels strongly that this is obviously equally important for the paying public. He cites an instance when a crucial part of the course was obliterated by a large advertising banner of the sponsoring petrol company. 'And I shall not be using that brand again,' he said over the air for thousands to hear. Needless to say, the offending banner was not placed in the same spot at subsequent meetings.

Brought up in Winchcombe surrounded by horses and educated at Cheltenham College, Peter Bromley had both endless riding on the Cotswolds and racing at National Hunt headquarters on his doorstep. Out riding, he never opened a gate when he could jump one and he found even hunting a bit tame. It was when he first went out to a fence to watch at Cheltenham that his life changed.

'I couldn't believe horses could jump fences at such speed,' he says. 'I went home, pulled up my leathers, practised and practised and from then on I was hooked.'

It was when his regiment was posted to Libya in 1952 that trainer Frank Pullen and jockey Tommy Cusack enticed him out of the army and into National Hunt racing. But it was not all plain sailing, for after only a month he suffered a fractured skull. He lay in his hospital bed listening to radio commentaries of racing and, thinking that a specialist was needed, there and then sowed the seeds for the future.

Then came the experiment by Lord March of Goodwood to use an in-race commentary along American lines. Soon racegoers were enjoying the smooth style and unhurried delivery of Bob Haynes's voice, followed by Michael Seth-Smith and Brian Firth. Gradually other courses took up the idea, and Peter Bromley, answering an advertisement, went for a trial, along with Colonel Tony Cooke, at Hurst Park.

Little could Peter Bromley know the significance of one of the races he read: it was the Triumph Hurdle, won by a certain Lester Piggott, landing a gamble on one of his few rides over hurdles.

From the start, Peter Bromley always had instant recall, and the ability to remember every detail when reading a race. With the company concerned, Broadcast Amplifiers of Brighton, later absorbed by Racecourse Technical Services, unable to decide between the two, Colonel Cooke, who went on to become ITV's first commentator,

and Peter Bromley were offered half a job each, which was 'better than nothing' at the time.

Travel was wide-ranging – there remains only Cartmel in all of England and Scotland that Peter Bromley has not been to. For commentating on all six races, he was paid £20 a day with no expenses. But it proved a marvellous foundation. The most important thing for a commentator, he says, is exceptional eyesight and the ability to *use* the eyes in conjunction with big, powerful binoculars. And naturally he does need a clear, uninterrupted view, which he certainly did not get one year when he was covering the Northumberland Plate at Newcastle, known as the Pitmen's Derby.

He was to commentate from a private box, but the friends of its owner did not realize the box was not available to them that day, and in they poured, chattering, pouring drinks and generally appearing paralytic. No one turfed them out, so Peter Bromley had to abandon his big binoculars – there was not enough elbow room to lift them up – and, with the microphone round his neck picking up the unwelcome 'noises off', he did his best. To his surprise no one complained about the quality of that commentary until Irish trainer Paddy Prendergast caught up with him, but he laughed when he heard the reason.

When Peter Bromley first had to wear glasses, he thought it would spell the end of his career. However, they have not caused serious problems, apart from when they steam up; then the only

The Triumph Hurdle at the now defunct Hurst Park in 1954 was Peter Bromley's first trial commentary race. The race was won by a youthful Lester Piggott.

thing to do is calmly wipe them in the middle of a race.

Immediate identification is imperative in commentating, so he has learned little tricks to help him along the way. One of the biggest problems is when an owner has given his jockey new colours; Peter cannot always see the runners in the paddock, and when he is used to a faded set, new ones can look like a totally different colour. Other problems can be caused when a jockey crouches low over his horse, masking crucial markings. An owner with two horses in a race is one thing, but these days an Arab owner can sometimes have four runners in a race and who wears which change of cap may be announced only half an hour before the race.

Apart from obscured races (and helicopters injudiciously parked can cause just as much obstruction as buses and banners), bad light is a nightmare for the commentator. The TV monitor which is in the commentator's box is fine as a last resort, but it can sometimes be fatal to take the eyes off the runners for even a split second. 'The most important thing is to eliminate panic, or the mind rats on you,' says Peter. 'I call it "relaxed tension": you have got to have the adrenalin and yet you also have to keep cool; your mind is

checking, checking all the time – it's awful when you are running through the field suddenly to see a horse you have already called!'

Peter does his homework overnight and for a big field he simply sits down and learns the names; it is also useful to memorize their draw, as it is rare for a horse to change completely from one side of the course to the other. The amount of mental effort that goes into race commentating is such that immediately afterwards he cannot remember what horses he has called. He very rarely goes out on a Friday night and four days of concentration at Royal Ascot leave him drained and exhausted – but he can enjoy the consolation of a job well done.

When Tony Cooke began ITV commentating, the BBC already had racing coverage by the great professional team of Peter O'Sullevan and the late Clive Graham; but *no* betting prices were given, either as an indication before the race or with the results afterwards. The new competition spurred the BBC on, and Peter Bromley came in as the third man, dealing with interviews and operating from a specially adapted Land Rover, complete with telephone, on the course. Betting was included for the first time, and Peter acted as a standby, should either of the others be unable to be present, and conducted interviews.

From there, he was appointed the BBC's first racing correspondent by Peter Dimmock (Fleet Street 'stringers' had been used previously), and for a time he had an office in both Broadcasting House and Television Centre, until he became full-time for radio, as he still is thirty years later. At that time, about fifty races a year were covered, more often big handicaps, but with the formation of the Pattern Race Committee, when Lord Porchester earmarked 100 or so races which justified group status, these became the broadcast races.

One of Peter Bromley's first jobs as BBC racing correspondent was to comment in 1960 on the Peppiatt Report, a government inquiry whose terms of reference were whether off-course betting should be legalized and whether a proportion of the money from it should go into racing. All day the newsroom handed Peter pages of the report for him to update and analyse.

It was really the forerunner of the Levy Board, but the Jockey Club refused to cooperate with the Peppiatt Committee, I have never understood why, except that they didn't want anyone interfering with 'their' sport.

It was another missed opportunity, having turned aside the chance to buy *all* racecourses immediately after the war for peanuts.

The legalization of off-course betting, enabling high street betting shops to open in 1961, was greatly to the benefit of bookmakers, of course,

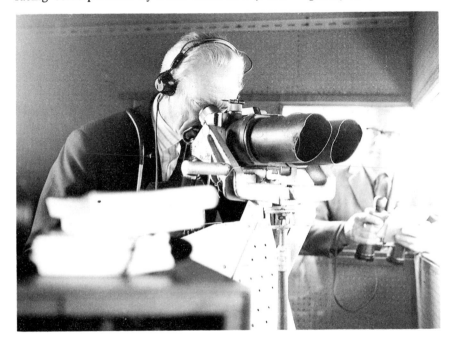

Peter O'Sullevan, doyen of the race commentary world, with his 'big eyes'.

but in return it was felt that they should contribute to the sport which enabled them to increase their livelihoods.

In 1961, the Levy Board came into existence under the chairmanship of Field Marshal Lord Harding, who had a fight on his hands with the bookmakers, trying to squeeze money out of them. They often failed to agree and a levy had to be imposed by the Home Secretary. Then came Lord Wigg – 'For all his faults he is fondly remembered,' says Peter Bromley – and he turned the whole thing round; instead of a levy on profits, there was to be a levy on a bookmaker's turnover.

It was this new money from betting into the sport that enabled many racecourses to carry out long overdue improvements and modernization, prize money to be increased and the Pattern system to be introduced. With the formation of the Levy Board, for the first time finances were no longer entirely in the hands of the Jockey Club. 'Subsequent chairmen tried to extract more for the sport, but the bookies were well organized.'

In the 1960s came the doping problems and, as a result of General Sir Randle Fielden's report, money for security was greatly increased, making both training and racecourse stables secure, introducing identification cards for stable staff and installing more patrol cameras and photo-finish equipment. Today, after witnessing more change in racing in thirty years than there had been in the previous 300 (and he rates a simple innovation like plastic rails one of the most important, for improving safety and making it possible to alter bends on courses), Peter Bromley believes the time has come for the power and finances of the industry to be integrated.

The best inquiry into the way that racing should go was the Benson Report in 1968. Among its many sensible recommendations was the setting up of a new statutory body to control and develop all aspects of the racing industry. Benson suggested the new body should be called the British Racing Authority. Racing has got too big for voluntary part-time amateurs; it is something like the sixth biggest industry in Britain after steel and coal, etc., and why should anyone give up three years of his life for nothing to be a Steward? They have much honest endeavour and are the best people to run the discipline side of racing; their conduct is above reproach.

But racing is a huge entertainment industry; the economics and finance of it should be run by a broader-based professional element, as Benson suggested.

But to implement Benson would have meant the Jockey Club losing its sovereignty; yet it made such good economic sense and would have made racing more commercial, but Benson was ahead of his time.

He adds: 'Racing should get the money it needs, and it should get it from betting. The removal of on-course betting tax has been a salvation and at last the crowds are coming back.'

He believes that overall prize money should not be allowed to fall below 50 per cent of the total cost of maintaining all racehorses in training, as recommended by Benson. The volume of prize money is the key to a prosperous racing and breeding industry but as yet no formula has been evolved that goes anywhere near satisfying that situation. 'I once owned a horse that won four races but it didn't earn its keep, and according to the statistical record, 95 per cent of all owners lose.'

All the professionals in racing, from the backroom boys and the stable lads upwards, should be amply rewarded and bigger prize money would benefit everyone.

The real imbalance, but one that is slowly sorting itself out, is between stud values and the rest of racing, making three-year-old winners of big races so valuable for stud that connections cannot afford to keep them in training at four or later, to the great detriment of spectators and racing as a whole. Peter Bromley would like to see the formation of a 'think tank' to find ways of solving problems like that, and of keeping horses in England.

The French sold all their best horses to America, and now their racing is in the doldrums, and the last time we had two generations of Derby winners clash in the King George at Ascot was Blakeney and Nijinsky in 1970.

A benefit of the Arabs in England is that they often keep older horses in training and many of them have bought studs in Britain and Ireland and stand their stallions there.

Peter Bromley does not favour centralization or Sunday racing.

I am a great supporter of small racecourses – they are part of the British character – but a lot are on the breadline and need local support. When they tried to close Edinburgh, Lord Rosebery mustered local support – they started National Hunt racing there – and now it is flourishing. A lot of it boils down to self-help, in terms of alternative uses on non-racing days such as golf courses in the centre and banquets or conferences in the buildings.

I am not mad about Sunday racing, I like my Sunday off with my wife and three daughters, and I don't believe it would be a great bonanza because of betting shops being closed. I think it would be a damp squib. There is too much racing on Saturdays as it is, and it becomes self-destructive.

(In December 1988 it was announced that an attempt to introduce Sunday racing on seven Sundays a year was to be made through a private

Armchair viewing has become an important part of racing thanks to expert TV coverage.

member's bill in the House of Commons, a move that was welcomed by many racecourses. When Ireland successfully started Sunday racing in 1985, Britain became the only major country not doing so, and other professional sports, including those which allow betting on their outcome, have been playing on Sundays for years.)

Of those who have held most power in his time in racing, Peter Bromley believes General Sir Randle Fielden did immense backroom work to get racing out of the doldrums. 'He may not have got all the credit he deserved, he did not court publicity, but he got on with the job. He won over the old guard at an important time and was not afraid. We need another one now.'

In its new Senior Steward, the forty-five-year-old Marquess of Hartington from Skipton, Yorkshire, it is to be hoped that the sport of kings has found just that.

'I Had a Tenner on!'

A Monday at Wolverhampton

It is a cold May Monday morning, a tweed-suit affair with, fortuitously, a coat thrown in at the last minute before heading off for Wolverhampton races.

The journey is an easy one, a series of roundabouts taking us ever closer to the town centre after turning off the M54. Past the Goodyear tyre factory on the left, and then the big gas works where we turn right, under a huge railway viaduct, and into the racecourse, bumping our way over the grass where just a handful of cars are already parked.

It is barely three-quarters of an hour before the first race, but the bookmakers are only just unpacking their boards and satchels from their not very young BMWs and Fords, while next door a smartly dressed couple sip coffee from a flask in the warmth of their car, which sports a racehorse mascot, its jockey in, presumably, the

Many Monday race meetings are staged strictly for the industry, to keep the betting shop business going; they also give small trainers a chance.

car occupants' colours. A toothless old boy with long, grey, bushy eyebrows, an old raincoat flapping over his baggy, tie-less dark suit and humped shoulders, helps direct the cars.

'Won't be much business today,' says one bookie. 'I'll definitely be packing up early.'

'Me too, mate,' says another from the adjacent motor car. 'Ten degrees colder here than at home.'

Thankful for the overcoat, the weekend's warm sunshine a rapidly receding memory, I make my way towards the tall, red-brick Victorian-looking buildings and the mid-1960s' members'/weighing-room complex, its flag aloft a cheering sign in large letters, 'Welcome to Dunstall Park'. The racecard seller stands stoically within his draughty kiosk. Normally he's a window cleaner. 'I don't know which is colder,' he says, but not in grumbling fashion.

A retired-colonel-type emerges from the champagne bar, walrus moustache pinned on to a florid complexion; he surely likes to keep warm from within. Welcome warmth is also at hand for me in the shape of the Dunstall Suite. The bulk of the club racegoers, it seems, are here. No wonder. Service at the bar and for a hot meal or sandwiches is good and the prices are not exorbitant. There is a Tote, and doors open on to a balcony in front and to the stands at the side. For one retired

Racing at Dunstall Park, which took over from Wolverhampton's first racecourse, Broad Meadows, in the 1880s.

Lily Langtry won the Dudley Plate with Montpensier at Wolverhampton in 1894, when she was still racing as 'Mr Jersey'.

couple, Frank and Mary Robson, this is the reason they never miss a meeting here.

They used to keep one or two horses with Fred Rimell, 'a marvellous man; he and Mercy were a great pair'. They recalled a day Terry Biddlecombe rode for them here at Wolverhampton, on a hard-pulling hurdler. Terry parted company at the second flight and the loose horse promptly jumped a chase fence. He won on his next outing, then sadly fell and broke his neck the next time.

'Yes, the sport's a great leveller,' says Frank Robson. 'It doesn't differentiate between royalty and the working man when it comes to things like that.' He tells a remarkable story. The chairman of his company once owned an unnamed three-year-old by Falcon out of a mare called Florence Nightingale. The ageing chairman, his health fading, had to sell him. 'He would have nearly given him to me,' Frank Robson recalls, 'but I was unable to take on the commitment at the time.' Before he died, the chairman named the gelding. He called him Night Nurse – and he went on to win the Champion Hurdle twice, as well as the Sweeps, Scottish and Welsh Champion Hurdles, then good steeplechases, and was second in the Cheltenham Gold Cup.

Now, on this cold May Monday, the Robsons have the day's form spread out on 'their' window table, plus sandwiches and a bottle of wine. Grandparents thirteen times over, they are settled in to enjoy their day, without any tinge of what might have been.

Signs of activity begin to take place outside, as the runners for the first race are taken across to the far side of the course for saddling. 'The number of runners is likely to exceed the spectators at a meeting like this,' clerk of the course, Lieutenant-Commander John Ford, had warned me in advance. The retired naval officer has held the reins here since 1972 and at Stratford-upon-Avon, that delightful home of the Horse and Hound Cup Final Champion Hunters Steeplechase, since 1974.

The fourteen runners cross over to the paddock, the bulk of which lies beside the sparsely populated silver ring, the top end in Tatts, a rather tired-looking flowerbed in the centre. The bookies start gesticulating odds; there seems to be a bigger crowd around the board giving a Tannoy of away racing, while the hot-dog van and cockles and mussels stall attract further trade.

The first race is a maiden auction guaranteed sweepstakes, over five furlongs, for two-year-old maidens at starting who must have been bought at public auction as yearlings in Great Britain or Ireland for 10,000 guineas or less. For every £750 paid under 10,000 guineas there is a 1-pound weight allowance down to a maximum of 12 pounds. Glancing at the card, I see there is only one horse, Tee Wall, claiming the full amount, making him, therefore, the cheapest horse in the race. I decide to keep an eye on him, but at odds of 33–1, it looks certain that the colt, owned by a Mr J. R. Smith and trained at Tamworth by Brian McMahon, will be an also-ran.

The brown colours with an orange diamond are easy to pick out. The five furlongs at Wolverhampton are straight and favour a high draw, according to racecourse information. Tee Wall, interestingly, is drawn highest at fourteen. Michael Wigham soon has him in a handy position, and as the final stages of the race take shape, he bursts into the lead – and there he stays for a convincing four-length shock win! The Tote pays 70–1.

Reporters gather round owner Rod Smith in the winner's enclosure. He has had horses in training for twenty years, and this is only his sixth win. A semi-retired newsagent, he is clearly in love with the game. 'It's my hobby. I've paid a lot of money through the nose, but since I've met Brian I've had more enjoyment than ever before. There are a lot of nice people about, or I wouldn't still be in the game. I'm a nobody.'

He paid 1000 Irish punts for Tee Wall, by French 2000 Guineas second Tampero out of a mare 'who did very little', Wallpark Princess. 'I had a tenner on,' says Mr Smith. 'I wish it had been more!' The favourite had been ridden into second place by Dana Mellor, one of the slowly growing band of woman professionals, and the younger daughter of Stan and Elaine Mellor.

Another woman, Julie Bowker, is riding in the second and she finishes third on a 25–1 outsider. It is the selling race, value £1000 and again over five furlongs. It has the smallest field of the day, just six runners, and provides the only clear-cut favourite of the afternoon to win, the filly Wasn't Me. She is trained by Jack Berry, fifth in Wolverhampton's 'league', and ridden by Ray Cochrane, third in the jockeys' equivalent. But although it is her second win, auctioneer David

Henson tries in vain to procure a bid for her in the ring afterwards. A chartered surveyor who is also clerk of the course and manager at Nottingham, it was the first no bid he had had for some time. 'In fact, I think the last time was this same horse,' he

Top *Broad Meadows, on which the lease expired in 1878, lay almost within the shadow of St Peter's Church.*

Above *Two of Wolverhampton's feature trophies, the Boar's Head Trophy (left) and the Pains Lane Trophy.*

confesses. 'There are some trainers who people seem to know not to bid against!'

The next two races are the nearest the day will come to any class, a three-year-old handicap over a mile for horses rated from 0–90 and a one mile one furlong fillies' stakes, also for three-year-olds but they must not have won a race worth £3500, both races valued at £3000. Now we start to see some of the better-known trainers, but it is a day, as Commander Ford explains, that is staged strictly for the industry.

> Such days are forced on us by the Levy Board, who then support us financially, to keep the betting shop business going. Otherwise, no one would want to stage such a meeting on a Monday, and they would have races open to £¼ million horses from top trainers. A day like this gives the small trainers a chance.
>
> We have to have conditions on the races, or we would quickly exceed the safety limit with the number of runners.

Wolverhampton's feature races in the year are the Harry Brown trophy, the Astbury trophy, Wolverhampton Champion Hurdle Trial and the Shrewsbury Cup.

Today, the handicap goes to another outsider, the 25–1 chance American-bred Tryneptune, ridden by stable lads' boxing champion Chris Rutter and trained by B. C. Morgan of Burton-on-Trent for Mrs Nicky Griffiths and Mrs N. G. G. Heritage. In all, there are twenty-three dually owned and six company-registered runners during the day. The 5–4 favourite, Main Objective, trained by Luca Cumani at Newmarket, finishes fourth, underlining professional punter Alex Bird's maxim never to back in handicaps.

In the eleven-runner fillies' race no fewer than eight are trained at Newmarket by such as Bill Jarvis, Michael Stoute, Henry Cecil (Wolverhampton's leading trainer), Geoff Wragg, Ron Sheather and Gavin Pritchard-Gordon. Owners include Sheikh Mohammed, who has horses with over twenty trainers in Britain, ship-owner Mr Stavros Niarchos and companies' director Sir Philip Oppenheimer, while jockeys include Bruce Raymond, Greville Starkey, Steve Cauthen and Pat Eddery.

Sheikh Mohammed's American-bred filly Lustre is the even-money favourite, but ends up dividing Henry Cecil's unraced pair, Steve Cauthen win-

Mr Harry Brown was the last amateur rider to become champion steeplechase jockey, in 1919. He was closely associated with Dunstall Park and was a director of the course from 1920 until 1958.

ning on Mrs J. W. Hanes's home-bred Bespoken, with Mr Niarchos's home-bred Azreill third.

Steve Cauthen is on the joint-favourite for the fifth race, a seven-furlong handicap, but it is Michael Wigham's day. He rides Glory Gold for Mel Brittain, the owner-trainer from Warthill, York, and the four-year-old filly shrugs off her 7-pound penalty for winning last time and gives Michael, who rode his first winner thirteen years earlier, a 254–1 double.

The last race is a one and a half-mile handicap, taking in the full extent of Wolverhampton's not unattractive, pear-shaped track, and with twenty-three runners it is the biggest field of the day. Top weight is Cabot, owned and bred by one of the most popular couples in racing, Mr and Mrs John Hislop, whose patience, skill and dedication were rewarded in the 1970s with their superb Brigadier Gerard, winner of the 2000 Guineas, King George, Eclipse Stakes, Champion Stakes twice, beaten only once in sixteen races.

As the runners mill round at the start, it is clear no jockey wants to hang about in the stalls too long; they are reluctant to move forward at the behest of starters Bill Rees, who as a National Hunt jockey won the Cheltenham Gold Cup on Pas Seul and partnered the crack two-miler Dunkirk in his ill-fated attempt to take on the mighty Arkle, and Mrs J. P. Grange, for fourteen years trainer's secretary to the late Bob Turnell.

'C'mon, get 'em up there,' urges Bill Rees sternly. 'Don't sit there doing nothing, get them going,' and Mrs Grange strides purposefully across to add weight to her chivvyings.

The six green-helmeted and -jacketed stalls handlers put their skill to good use on one recalcitrant, narrowly avoiding its lashing hind legs. With the aid of a hood blindfolding him, and special straps behind him, he is soon loaded and, to the bookmakers' last coaxings of the day, the runners surge off to a perfect even break.

A cheer goes up when joint-favourite Tancred Walk, ridden by Paul Cook, streams first past the post ahead of three outsiders. It hasn't been a good day for punters – or tipsters.

In three of the six races, all thirteen national newspaper tipsters failed to pick the winner. Just three picked Glory Gold; only one chose Tancred Walk, but he had napped him; and it was only the six-horse seller which produced nine tips for the winner and the remaining four for the runner-up.

So had the bookies had a good day? 'No, it was too cold,' said one. 'But we've won.'

It was the same story from the man at the sweet stall.

'You're about my second customer, luv,' he says, as I purchase a bar of chocolate for the homeward trip. 'It won't pay today. It's not summery enough yet,' implying optimistically that before long it will be.

He has travelled from Wakefield in Yorkshire, 'but the motorways make it easy', and as he pops across to the bookies for a bet, it's clear he too is here because he loves it. 'Yes, I've got a horse in partnership and I go to as many meetings as I can ...'

Soon there is little left but the inevitable litter blowing around the tarmac, as that day's Wolverhampton racegoers join the queue of cars leaving. As Frank and Mary Robson said, 'We have lots of fun. We love it.'

Bibliography

Alex Bird, the Life and Secrets of a Professional Punter
Alex Bird with Terry Manners, Macdonald Queen Anne Press 1985

Arkle, the Story of a Champion
Ivor Herbert, Pelham Books 1966

Cheltenham Racecourse
Alan Lee, Pelham Books 1985

Directory of the Turf
Pacemaker Publications, various editions

Epsom Racecourse
David Hunn, Davis Poynter 1973

Fred Archer, His Life and Times
John Welcome, Faber and Faber 1967

Great Racing Disasters
John Welcome, Arthur Barker 1985

Headquarters, the History of Newmarket and Its Racing
Richard Onslow, Great Ouse Press 1983

The History of Steeplechasing
Michael Seth-Smith, Peter Willett, Roger Mortimer, John Lawrence, Michael Joseph 1966

Horse Racing
Peter Churchill, Blandford Press 1981

Horse Racing
Dennis Craig, J.A. Allen 1949

Horse Racing, the Inside Story
Noel Blunt, Hamlyn 1977

Infamous Occasions
John Welcome, Michael Joseph 1980

Julian Wilson's 100 Greatest Racehorses
Julian Wilson, Macdonald Queen Anne Press 1987

Knavesmire
John Stevens, Pelham Books 1984

Lester Piggott, the Pictorial Biography
Julian Wilson, Macdonald Queen Anne Press 1985

Men and Horses I Have Known
The Hon. George Lambton, Thornton Butterworth 1924

My Story
Sir Gordon Richards, Hodder and Stoughton 1955

Old Country Silver
Margaret Holland, David and Charles 1971

The Price of Success, the Authorized Biography of Ryan Price
Peter Bromley, Hutchinson/Stanley Paul 1982

Racing Reflections
John Hislop, Hutchinson 1955

Ruff's Guide to the Turf and The Sporting Life Annual
The Sporting Life, various editions

The Sporting Life Results and Trainers Reviews, Flat and National Hunt Seasons
The Sporting Life, various editions

The Story of Tattersall's
Peter Willett, Stanley Paul 1987

Summerhays' Encyclopaedia for Horsemen
Warne 1952

Vincent O'Brien's Great Horses
Ivor Herbert and Jacqueline O'Brien, Pelham Books 1984

Index

Page numbers in *italic* refer to the
illustrations

Aboyeur, 51–2
Aga Khan, 22, 33
Albert House Stables, 58, *59*, 60
Aldaniti, 91, *91*
Alleged, 118–19, 131
Ambush II, 12
Amour Drake, *73*
Anmer, 51
Anne, Princess Royal, 13, *13*, 20, *22*, *90*
Anne, Queen, 12, 44, *44*
April the Fifth, 19
Arabs, 8, 33–5, 77–8, 149, 166
Archer, Fred, *12*, 23–8, *23*, *25–8*, 83–4,
    124, 127
Archer, Nelly Rose, 27–8
Ardross, 49
Arkle, 43, 80, 135–9, *136*, *138–9*
Armstrong, Robert, 19
Arnull, John, 16
Arnull, Sam, 16
Arnull, William, 17
Ascot, 12, 44–52, *45–52*
Ashmahl, 151
Asmussen, Cash, 51, 52, *134*
Assert, 119
Astor, Waldorf, 33
At Talaq, 125
Aureole, 84

Baezo, Braulio, 118
Bahram, 33
Balding, Ian, 19
Ballymoss, *112*, 113
The Bard, 25
Barlow, Mrs J., *149*
Bayardo, 49, 55
Bend Or, 25–6, *27*
Benson Report, 166
Bentinck, Lord George, 29, 30–1, 97–9,
    98, 105
Beresford, Lord William, 63
betting, 64–70, 71–4, 165–6
Big Game, 12
Bird, Alex, 71–4, *71*, *74*, 75, 172
Blanchard, 26
bookmakers, 64–70, 165–6
Brabazon, Aubrey, 112
Bradley, Kim, *151*
Bridget, 15
Brigadier Gerard, 135, 172
Briscoe, Basil, 93–5
British School of Racing, 157–61,
    157–61
Bromley, Peter, 19–20, 162–7, *163*
Brown, Harry, *172*
Brown Jack, 49, 84
Bucephalus, 43
Buck House, *153*, 154, 156
Buckle, Frank, 17, 130
Bunbury, Sir Charles, 14–15, *15*, 16, 22, 41
Burnborough, 125–6
Burrough Hill Lad, 93
Butler, Rab, 69
Byerley Turk, 8–9, 44

Cadland, 17
Calder, Doreen, 142, 144–7, *146*
The Callant, 142

Carabineer, *151*
Carbine, 124, *125*
Carrozza, *132*, 133
Cauthen, Steve, 131–2, 172
Cecil, Henry, 129, 131, 158, 172
Chamier, 113
Champion, Bob, *87*, 91, *91*
Chandler, Victor, 76, 78
Charles, Prince of Wales, 8, 46
Charles II, King, 7–·8, 12, 14
Chester, 10, *10*
Chirol, Michel, 152
Clark, Tony, 51
Cloister, 72
Cochrane, Ray, 20, 21–2
Coleman, Thomas, 89
Commanche Run, 131
El Conquistador, 51
Cooke, Tony, 163–4, 165
Cottage Rake, 112
Count Shazariee, *150*
Craganour, 51–2
Crisp, 91, 122, *123*
Crockford, William, 99
Crucifix, 30–1
Cumani, Luca, 59–60
Cumberland, William, Duke of, 12, 39, *40*

Daglish, Bruce, 107
Dancing Brave, 79, 116
Darley Arabian, 8–9, 44
Darling, Fred, 78–9, 84
Davison, Emily, 51
Dawn Run, 135, 152–6, *153–6*
Dawson, Matt, 24, 25, 26
Day, Sam, 17
Deane, Gerald, 33, 35
Delaneige, 93–4
Derby, 14–22, *16–22*, 25, 33, 43, 46,
    51–2, *65*, *68*, 78–9, 101–3, *102*, *116*
Derby, Lord, 14–15, *14*
Desert Orchid, *153*
Devon Loch, 13, 91, *92*, 112
Diamond Jubilee, 12
Dickinson, Michael, 53–4, 55, 56–7, 146
Diomed, 15, *15*, 16–17, 22
Distel, 80
Donoghue, Steve, 84
Doyoun, 20–1
Dreaper, Tom, 135, 136, 137–8, *139*
Dunlop, John, 158

Earl's Brig, 144
Early Mist, 112
Easterby, M.H., 101
Easterby, Mick, 53
Eclipse, 12, 14, 17, 30, 39–43, *39*, *42*
Edward VII, King, 12, *12*, *13*, 63
Elis, 105
Elizabeth, Queen Mother, 13, 20, *22*,
    46, 91
Elizabeth, II, Queen, 13, 20, 22, 46, *50*,
    52, 84, *85*, 133
Emblem, 91
Emblematic, 91
Empire Rose, *126*
Epsom, 14–22, *16–22*, 46, *65*

Falmouth, Lord, 24, 26
Fielden, General Sir Randle, 166, 167
Flying Ace, 144–7, *146*
The Flying Dutchman, 135
Flying Fox, 32, 33, *34*
Flyingbolt, 135, 138
Foinavon, 91

Ford, John, 170, 172
Fordham, George, 24, 84
Four Legged Friend, 60
Freddie, 142
Fry, Dick, 69
Fry, Sidney, 67, 69

Galbreath, John, 117–18
Gay Future, 97
Gaye Brief, 152, 153–4
George IV, King, 12, 46
George V, King, 12, 51
George VI, King, 12
Gildoran, 51
Glacial Storm, 20, 21, *21*
Gladiateur, 49
Gladness, 113
Godolphin Arabian, 9, 44
Gold Cup (Ascot), 49–52
Golden Fleece, 117, 119
Golden Miller, 80, *81*, 91, 93–5, *94*, 135
Good Hand, 97
Goodwood, 162, *162*, 163
El Gran Señor, 119, *119*
Grand National, *81*, 86–95, *86–94*
Gray, Kevin, 151
Griffin, Harry, 61–2
Griffiths, Major Barney, 157, *157*,
    160–1, *160*
Grimthorpe, Dowager Lady, 67–8
Guest, Raymond, 115

Hamlyn, Geoffrey, 70, 75–82, *75*
Hancock, Bull, 113, 116
Handsome Sailor, 48–9
Hannibal, 17
Hartigan, Paddy, 84
Harvester, 17
Hatton's Grace, 112, 135
Hay, Adam, 145, 147
Hayes, Colin, 122, 125
Hello Gorgeous, 33, 37
Herod, 9, 12, 43
Highbrow, 52
Highflyer, 30, *30*, 43
Hill, Charmian, 152–6, *155*
Hill, William, 70, 78–9, *79*
Hill House, 101
Hills, Barry, 53, 54–6, *55*, 56, 57
Hindley, C., 16
Hislop, John, 172
Hobbs, Bruce, 58, 60
Holland-Martin, Tim, 49
Hutchinson, Ron, 120–1, *121*, 125
Hyperion, 69

Ile de Chypre, 52, *52*
Imman, *149*
In The Money, 97
Insurance, 80
Intermezzo, 121, *121*
Iroquois, 25
Isinglass, 49

Jacamar, 52
James I, King, 10, 12
Jay Trump, 142
Jockey Club, 12, 30, 33, 38, 52, 61, 64,
    67, 69, 96–103, 134, 165, 166

Kahyasi, 20, 21–2, *21*, *22*, 33, 60, 105
Kerim Bey, *150*
Knock Hard, 112

Ladbrokes, 69, 78, 82

The Lamb, 91
Langtry, Lily, *169*
Lawson, Joe, 33, 56
Le Moss, 49
Leander, 99
Levy, Goodman, 97–9
Levy Board, 89, 96–7, 166, 172
Loates, Tom, 62, *62*
Lottery, 43, 89
Lynn, William, 88
Lyphard, 33

Maccabeus, 97–9
McCourt, Graham, *87*
McLoughlin, Liam, 136
Magic Milly, 60
Mahmoud, 22, 33
Maksud, 19, 20, 21
Al Maktoum, Sheikh Hamdan, 20, 21,
   29, 77, 125, *151*
Manifesto, 91, 135
Manton, 33, 53–7, *54–7*
Margaret, Princess, *50*
Marrian, Dr G.F., 101
Marshall, Bryan, 112
Matchem, 43
Melbourne Cup, 120–1, *120*, *122*,
   124–5, *126*
Mellor, Dana, 170
Merry, Kevin, 60
Merryman, 142–3
Mill House, 135, 136–7, 138
Mill Reef, 19, 33, 135
Minoru, 12
The Minstrel, 113, *115*, 118, 131
Minting, 25
Miss Boniface, 52
Moifaa, 91
Mont Tremblant, 80
Montrose, Duchess of, *12*, 27
Morris, Mouse, 59
Mtoto, 105, *106*
Al Mufti, 20, 21
Al Muhalhal, 21
Mulcahy, Jack, 113
Muley Edris, 25
Mullins, Tony, 153, 156
Mulvey, Sean, 157
Murless, Noel, 129–30
My Virginian, 96

National Stud, *11*
Natski, *126*
Nelson, Charlie, 53
Never Say Die, *128*, 129
Newmarket, 7–8, *7–9*, 10–12, *11*, *12*, 29,
   31, 38, 58
Night Nurse, 170
Nijinsky, 33, 113–15, 116–17, *117*, *118*,
   119, 130, *130*, 166
Nimbus, *73*
No Bombs, 101
Northern Dancer, 29, 116

Oakley, John, 41, *42*
The Oaks, 15
O'Brien, David, 119
O'Brien, Vincent, 29, 33, *38*, 111–19,
   111–19, 130, 131
O'Kelly, Colonel, 17, 41, 43
O'Neill, Jonjo, 153, *155*, 156
Ormonde, 25, *26*
O'Sullevan, Peter, 78, *165*

Paget, Dorothy, 77, *77*, 80, *81*, 93, *94*, 95

Parker, Max, 78
Partner, 9
Patron, 17
Peppiatt Report, 165
Persimmon, 12, *13*, 32, 49
Phar Lap, 124, *125*
Piggott, Lester, 22, 23, 24, 25, 49, 84,
   115–16, *116*, 117–18, 127–34, *127–34*,
   163, *165*
Piggott, Susan, 129, 133–4, *133*
Pinturischio, 69
Pinza, 84, *85*
Pitman, Richard, *100*
Porter, John, 25, 32, 79
Posada, 49
Prescott, Sir Mark, 59
Priam, 17
Price, Ryan, 101, 130
Prince Regent, 135
Psidium, 56

Quare Times, 112

Racecourse Security Services, 96–103
Rank, Mrs J.V., 77, 80
Ratan, 99
Red Glow, 20, 21
Red Handed, 124
Red Keidi, 96
Red Rum, *90*, 91, 122, 135, 147
Rees, Bill, 173
Rheingold, 117, 118
Ribero, 116, 130
Richards, Gordon, 23, 79, 83–4, *83*, *85*,
   129
Riordan, John, 152
Robert the Devil, 25, *27*
Roberto, 117–18, 130
Roberts, Michael, 19, 20
Robinson, David, 33
Robinson, Jem, 130–1
Robinson, Willie, 137
Robson, Robert, 79
Rogers, Sam, 99
Roman Hackle, 80
Rose of England, 84
Rous, Admiral, 64
Royal Gait, 49–52, *51*
Royal Palace, 116, 130
Royal Tan, 112
Run and Skip, *154*, 155
Running Rein, 97–9, *98*

Sadeem, 51, 52
Sagaro, 49
St Cloud, 63
St Gatien, 17
St Leger, Anthony, 15
St Martin, Yves, *102*, 103
St Mirren, 27
St Simon, 25, 49
Sangster, Robert, 29, 33, 53–4, *54*, 56,
   113, 124, 130, 131
Saraband, 25
Sassoon, Sir Victor, 84
Scargill, Dr Jon, 58–60, *60*
Sceptre, *31*, 32, 80
Scott, Archie, 64, *64*, 66–70, 75, 78
Scott, Brough, 84
Scott, Charlie, 142
Seagram, 89
Secreto, 119, *119*
Sergeant, 17
Shahrastani, 33, 117
Shergar, 33, 131

Sheriff's Star, 20, 21
Sievier, Robert, 32, *80*
Sir Harry Lewis, 54
Sir Ivor, 113–16, *116*, 119, 130, 133
Sir Thomas, 12
Sloan, Tod, 61–3, *61*, *62*
Smiles, Peter, 96–7, *96*, 99–100, 103
Smith, Tommy, 142
Sno Serenade, 20
Solario, 33
Solford, 80
Spion Kop, 66, *66*
Sporting Life, 76–7
Starkey, Greville, 52, *52*
Stein family, 78
Stevens, George, 24, 91
Stoute, Michael, 53
Straight Deal, 80
Sun Chariot, 12
Superpower, 49
Surplice, 31
Surtees, R.S., 141, 142
Swannell, David, 83, 84
Swiss Maid, 33
Sylvan Tempest, 20

Taaffe, Pat, 112, 137–8
Tancred Walk, 173
Tattersall's, 29–38, *30–2*, *34–8*, 56,
   64
Taylor, Alec, 33, 53, 80
Tee Wall, 170
Teenoso, 131, *131*
Tenea, 33
Thatch, 113
Thomond II, 93, 94, 95
Thomson, Lady, 135, 136, 137, 138–9
Todd, George, 56
Tommy Tittlemouse, 27
Topham, Mirabel, 88, 91–3
Tosetti, John, 23, 28, 83–4
Tote, 66, *67*, 69,70, 78
Troy, 101
Tudor Minstrel, 78–9, *79*
Tweedie, Reg, 142, 144

Unfuwain, 20, 21

Vaguely Noble, 32, 33, *34*, 116
Victoria, Queen, 12, 30, 46
Voltigeur, 135

Waajib, 20
Wasn't Me, 170–2
Watt, Michael, 29, 33–6, *35*, 37, 38
Watts, Bill, 53
Weatherby family, 30
Weir, Lady, 101
West Australian, 49
Westminster, Anne, Duchess of, 136,
   137, 139, *139*
Westminster, 1st Duke of, 25
Wigham, Michael, 172
Wildman, William, 39–41
Wilkinson, Sue, 151
Williams, Robert, 59
Wilson, Gerry, 93–4, *94*, 95
Winter, Fred, *87*, 142
Wood, Charles, 99

York, 9, 10
York, Duchess of, 46, *50*
Young Eclipse, 17

Zarathustra, 49